Caroline Kautsire is originally from Malawi, Africa, and is currently an English literature and writing professor at Bunker Hill Community College and Bay State College in Boston. She has published poetry and flash fiction that explores themes such as searching for identity, struggling with intimacy, and learning to love. Also a stage actress and director, Caroline was nominated for best-supporting actress by the Eastern Massachusetts Association of Community Theatres for her performance as Trinculo in William Shakespeare's *The Tempest*. She also teaches public speaking and has given several inspirational talks at colleges in Boston.

To my parents, Lilian Doreen Kautsire and Montfort Ben Kautsire, for their love and support. To my brothers, Charles Joseph Kautsire and Trevor Christopher Kautsire, for encouraging me to see and think positively. And, finally, to God, for saving my life and giving me a second chance to write this wonderful book which I hope will change many lives.

Caroline Kautsire

WHAT KIND OF GIRL?

AN AFRICAN CHILD CAUGHT BETWEEN WORLDS

AUSTIN MACAULEY PUBLISHERS™

LONDON • CAMBRIDGE • NEW YORK • SHARJAH

Ordering Information:
Quantity sales: special discounts are available on quantity purchases by corporations, associations, and others. For details, contact the publisher at the address below.

Publisher's Cataloging-in-Publication data
Kautsire, Caroline
What Kind of Girl?

ISBN 9781647502225 (Paperback)
ISBN 9781647502232 (Hardback)
ISBN 9781647502249 (ePub e-book)

Library of Congress Control Number: 2020905032

www.austinmacauley.com/us

First Published (2020)
Austin Macauley Publishers LLC
40 Wall Street, 28th Floor
New York, NY 10005
USA

mail-usa@austinmacauley.com
+1 (646) 5125767

I want to thank Emerson College for inspiring me to write a meaningful memoir with honesty and precision. I thank Jerald Walker, Daniel Tobin, Pamela Painter, Maria Flook and my writing workshop classmates for awakening the writer in me. To my mentor, Steven Dooner, for being an incredible friend and advisor who never gave up on me but believed in my potential to produce a good book and to be someone inspirational. To my friend and former colleague, Thomas Olivieri, for being a good listener and helper.

Table of Contents

"Oh, *Hell* No!"

You've probably heard the expression before: "Oh, *hell* no!" I had first heard it in Malawi, when I was watching American television, and quickly learned how to communicate it with attitude. On T.V., the people who used the expression were usually African-American women, swirling their heads in a circular motion, one finger wagging in the air to emphasize how they did not want to be "messed with." By the time I was six, I decided that I wanted to be the kind of girl who wasn't messed with either. If I was caught doing the American gesture, my father always likened me to my grandmother who was notorious for being a woman who wouldn't be told "no," even when she smoked in the hospital room on the day I was born.

During one of our long car rides together, my father described it all to me. I was a newborn baby battling clouds of smoke from my grandmother's cigarette. He told me how she stood there, wearing a chitenje and African headwrap, in a dark corner of the hospital room, like a powerful Mafia Godfather, spewing predictions that I would be a difficult child by the sound of my cries. My mother held me in her arms and did her best to wave away the smoke. She was mildly distracted and nervous as she peered outside the window, hoping my father would arrive to see me for the first time. Outside, the heavy rains of January came down in Lilongwe, Malawi, and made the dirt roads to Nkhoma Hospital too muddy for safe travel. Nevertheless, my father's white Peugeot 405 swerved dangerously back and forth along the roads as he made his unsteady way to me. At one point, the car spun a full one-eighty, turning him back to the direction from which he came, but despite nature's fair warning about what was to come, he did not allow these premonitory storms to stop him.

Discovering that I had endured unceasing secondhand smoking as an infant fascinated me. I imagined a baby with smokeproof lungs, and I needed to know more about this. By the time I turned six, my father would patiently field a thousand questions from his overly inquisitive daughter.

"Dad, but why didn't you tell her to smoke somewhere else?" I would ask, whenever we drove around town. My voice was always covered with concern but sometimes I shrieked as if I was accusing him of bad parenting.

"People asked her to smoke outside, but she never listened to anyone," he would say, laughing. His chuckles were light but behind their playfulness, I often traced a deep stare which he cast straight through the windshield at the road ahead, as if he could see his mother smoking right in front of him.

"Eh, your grandmother was a very stubborn woman."

Car rides were bonding time for my father and me. We were usually accompanied by the songs of our favorite Indian musician, Daler Mehndi, whose drum rhythms resembled African music. Because my father had many

Indian friends, he developed a taste for that music. During our drives, we bobbed our heads to Mehndi's songs from his album *Dardi Rab Rab*, a cassette I played obsessively each time I got into the car. Sometimes my father would try to change the tape to his favorite classical music, but at the sight of his reaching hand, I would transform into a puppy version of the three-headed dog, Cerberus, guarding the cassette player with an agitated glare, ready to pounce on anyone who tried to tamper with my precious Indian songs. Sometimes I danced around in the passenger seat while touching my index fingers to my thumbs, twisting them to the rhythm of songs in the style of Indian music videos. When my father and I sang along, we mimicked the sound of Indian words but what came out of us was nonsense. When others heard us sing, they gave our performance doubtful looks, but my father and I sang with pride. We would smile at each other, our faces beaming, heads still bobbing, content with our efforts to utter words we did not understand. This worked for us. This was father-daughter bonding, an original thing that set us apart from how other Malawians connected with each other.

In the middle of our jam sessions, my father told me about my grandparents—how strict his father was about manners, that when he disciplined a child, he made sure he gave them something to cry about. Grandfather's nostrils would flare open, eye squinted and firmly piercing, as if he were about to perform an exorcism on whomever he was screaming at. A face I had seen my father make, too, when I misbehaved. Grandfather was a man who believed in morals, education, and providing for his family. The kind of man who glorified Malawian culture and shunned any hanky-panky business that strayed from the norm. During our car rides, my father would recount stories about grandfather's wrath and morals, anything that would help me understand how he was brought up, anything to help me understand the evolution of the Kautsire family.

"You would feel like burying yourself if he yelled at you," my father said, popping his dark brown eyes with the look of someone who remembers horrors. I knew many Malawians who were strict like my grandfather, but my grandmother was the opposite. In a society where women were expected to be passive and submissive, she was opinionated about everything, ready to fling hard responses at anyone who tried to restrict her from doing things outside of the norm. No wonder why the woman smoked around a newborn baby. One could say my grandparents were the perfect combination of yin and yang. Either that or a difficult mixture of water and oil.

As my father and I drove through the streets of Blantyre and Limbe, he also told me stories about selling worms to European fishermen during his childhood. Since I only knew my father as a successful insurance man who always wore suits and ties and worked in a big office, it was difficult to imagine him selling worms, let alone touching them. My father's childhood was far off to me, a phase of his life when he used his bare hands to dig in the mud for worms just to make a little money for school. For a six-year-old living in Malawi, where snakes are a common fear for many and where rumors about black mambas lurking in houses spread like wildfire, it wasn't long before I embellished the story about my father's worm business. To my young mind, worms were snakes. A person had to be brave to touch snakes which, according to me, were always out to bite people. So even though my father sought the danger by digging them up in the first place, I saw him as a man with guts. Maybe he was even stubborn like my grandmother. I had a better way of telling his story. My family legend was forged and ready: "Dad sold tiny snakes for school money." That way, my father and I had something in common about our childhood—I was an infant who survived cigarette smoke, and dad was a survivor of tiny snakes.

The stories my father told me in the car were like African folktales, and some of them featured my life. I enjoyed hearing about myself as a baby—savoring the odd idea that I had a life I could not put to memory. My grandmother died before I could build memories of her too, so I never had the comforting *anganga* (or nana) experience. Just like that distant baby Caroline, I wanted to know more about who she was. She was another woman who seemed to say "Oh, *hell* no!" to anything that stifled her wishes. Our stories seemed like two parts of one mystery of a past time, and I saw how my father became a different man when he talked about his mother. Whenever he spoke of her, his laughter sounded raw, purer than other times, and his eyes glowed—still staring at the windshield as though he were watching movie scenes of his mother.

I laughed about my grandmother smoking around me too.

"You were crying in your mother's arms and *there* was *my* mother, puffing on a cigarette," he pressed two fingers on his lips, imitating how she placed the cigarette in her mouth. "The room was filled with smoke!" He swayed his head around as if the smoke were in the car.

We used to laugh about it, my father and I. It excited me to have an outrageous grandmother. In Malawi, smoking women automatically inherited a reputation for mischief. It was rare for black Malawian women to smoke but more common for mixed-race women whom we often called "colored people." "Coloreds" were not thought of as black. They were closer to whites, so it was acceptable for mixed-race women to smoke as they seemed more privileged than blacks. Coloreds could do with Malawian culture as they wished. Although my father knew it was unhealthy for his mother to smoke around his newborn baby, I suspect he laughed because he enjoyed reminiscing about who she was, even if some of the stories he told were about her bad habits. From what I heard, my grandmother was a stubborn woman who did not want to be told what to do—the kind of woman you might find sitting in the corner of a kitchen, smoking while cooking. Sometimes, in my imagination, she would sit with her arms folded, a cigarette in one hand, and a challenging look on her face that read, "Try messing with me and see what happens!" In my head, she was the kind of woman who was stubborn for the sake of stubbornness, or maybe her attitude was the result of being suffocated by too many questions about women in Malawian culture. Or perhaps she was the kind of woman who was unsatisfied with fickle female behavior. I'm sure she had her reasons, but one thing was certain: she was rebellious and defiant— I had a very bad-ass grandmother who wouldn't take any crap from people—Oh, *hell* no!

As I grew older, I still laughed about how she smoked around me when I was a baby, but I had other pressing questions: why didn't anyone *drag* her out of the hospital room? Shouldn't there have been some kind of protocol on smoking in hospitals? Sometimes, when I got in trouble for mischief, my parents yelled at me and warned me with possible punishment. My comebacks, which I used partly to guilt-trip my parents and partly to tug at their sympathy, often involved dropping cheeky remarks, like how I was screwed up in the head because of the smoke I inhaled at birth.

*

One evening, I ran into the kitchen and found my mother cooking dinner. She stood in silence at the stove, her African wrap, a *chitenje*, wrapped around her waist over her dress. I must have been seven or eight years old, very eager to show her the new gesture I had learned from black women on television. I remembered my mission to perform for my mother a scene from *The Cosby Show,* where Clair Huxtable explained to a boy that she did not serve her husband as a servant but that she performed tasks for him out of love. It was her way of articulating that women were not secondary to men. I liked the idea because I had observed Malawian women cooking and cleaning without the help of men. It seemed unfair that in a household where an entire family lives, chores were not divided equally. I had seen both men and boys sit comfortably while females ran around cleaning, fetching things for them, preparing breakfast, lunch, and dinner. I saw it in our home too, even though we had a houseboy to do most of the work. I didn't mind doing things for my two teenage brothers, Charles and Trevor, but I hated being ordered to cater to them when they weren't even busy. I would be stuck stirring chicken stew in the kitchen while Charles laid on his bed playing Nintendo video games and Trevor would be striking a million poses in the mirror, trying on new clothes he picked up from a store. I found it unfair, but no matter how often I protested this Malawian tradition, my little voice went unheard. All I could do was mutter sarcastic remarks under my breath, knowing my words were as good as silence. American television showed me something different about domestic life. Women stood up to men. They were not afraid to tell them off, not afraid to ask men for help.

"Ma!" I shrieked, startling her as she stirred the *ndiwo*, beef stew, at the stove. "Look! *Look*!"

Before she could ask if everything was okay, I struck a pose—legs apart, one hand on my hip, and another pointed at the ceiling. "Oh, *hell* no!" I shouted, swirling my head as smoothly as I could. The head and neck movement felt awkward, robotic. I probably looked like a broken machine jerking around, struggling to revive fluid motion.

My mother burst into laughter with a deep wide smile, and eyes squinted; her cheekbones rose, shining from a combination of the kitchen light and the heat from the stove.

"What is that, Carol?"

I snickered, still holding my pose. "That's how you say *no*," I said. Then I did it again.

She chuckled harder, wiping her forehead with her chitenje. I loved making her laugh. It was better than watching her stir food on the stove in silence. I always wonder if she knew, at that time, what I meant by, "That's how you say *no*." I don't think I fully understood my own context either, but I know I liked the idea of a woman having the ability to say "no" when something didn't sit well with her. I would soon learn another American expression, "Oh no, you di'nt!" Throughout my childhood, my normal pronunciation waxed and waned between British and Malawian accents because the schools I attended were influenced by British style English. But on top of this, I practiced saying the expressions with an American accent because of all the television I watched. American expressions sounded better if I tried to put on an authentic American accent and a fierce attitude. I liked sounding like someone who didn't easily give into things.

My mother enjoyed my performances because she knew I loved mimicking strong females on T.V., and she approved as long as I wasn't being disrespectful. Sometimes, if my father saw me doing the "*Hell* no!" gesture, he would watch me with a skeptical eye, probably wondering whom I was addressing in my little mind. Sometimes, he stared at me in a peripheral view, shaking his head with the look of a person who was distrustful of anything I might have said or did. He never knew what to make of my T.V. attitudes because they were not part of Malawian culture. The gestures were too confrontational for a well-behaved Malawian female and for some reason, I wanted to test the waters with my unusual behavior. Aside from months of bothering my friends, brothers, and cousins with my American head-swirls, I also targeted my father with spontaneous performances of my expressions, especially when he was reading his newspaper in the living room. I positioned myself in a space near him, usually in the dining room, which was adjacent to our living room. While pretending to grab a tangerine from the dining room table, I watched him from the corner of my eye, hoping he was aware of my presence. Then, just as he flipped the newspaper, I would strike my signature pose with one hand on my hip, as if an imaginary friend had provoked me. "Oh, *hell* no!" I shouted out of nowhere, swirling my head and wagging my finger. Then I waited for my father to react. He would look at me for a second, then, with soft chuckles, dismiss everything either as television nonsense or regard them as another permutation of the stubbornness I had inherited from my grandmother.

I was stubborn too and still am. It irked me when people told me what to do. At six years old, when my mother tried to teach me how to tie a chitenje around my waist, I hated everything about it. The fabric looked too colorful, too bright. The creative patterns and embroideries looked too complicated and ugly, as if a child had scribbled wildly on fabric. One day, my mother and I were sitting in my bedroom when she stood up from my bed and unraveled a chitenje. She held it horizontally behind her at waist-level. My mother had a full-figured body with wide hips and thighs. Her arms stretched out the chitenje rigidly to ensure I had a clear view of every step. She wrapped the left half over her dress, then around her waist.

"Bring this other side here," she said, overlapping the left half with the right. "Then tuck the edge of it on your hip. Make sure it's firm enough to hold up the chitenje. You don't want it falling down in front of people, especially if you aren't wearing anything under it." We both snickered at the thought of a chitenje unraveling and exposing a naked body in public.

It looked simple, similar to wrapping a towel around my waist. I tried the same steps but, unlike my mother, I was very skinny. It wrapped around me more than once, and I felt like an Egyptian mummy. Everything was imbalanced as I looked at it in the mirror. The chitenje reached above my belly button and since I was short, it also covered my legs, making it difficult for me to walk. I removed it immediately and threw it across the room.

"I hate chitenjes!" I shouted.

"But girls need to wear chitenjes sometimes. When cooking, cleaning, you can cover yourself with it." In Malawian culture, chitenjes are worn to cover women's legs. It is a sign of respect when moving around in public. I also learned very quickly that showing skin was like a mating call, a green light for sex. Therefore, the less skin you showed the better. With a chitenje, you can maneuver around the streets like a well-mannered female.

"But they're ugly!" I protested, hiding the fact that I was annoyed because it didn't wrap around me well. "And I hate cooking." I threw myself on the bed and lay on my belly, hands wrapped above my head.

"Then you are not a good girl, Carol," she said in a soft voice that begged me to reconsider. She sat on my bed and rubbed my back. "What kind of girl doesn't cook?"

I didn't know. And for a moment, I wanted to ask her to tell me the answer to her question, but I didn't want to sound rude, like I was challenging her. Instead, I spoke from the cocoon I had created with my arms. "Ma, I get burnt all the time when I cook," I sniffled as if I were sobbing. "I don't like it."

My many failed attempts to wrap a chitenje sealed my hatred for African attire. Whether it was dresses, shorts, shirts, or head-wraps, if I saw traces of bright fabric with intricate patterns, I automatically did not like it. The beauty of African apparel was lost on me, especially because older men and women wore them more often than young people. Some women wore them around their waists and chests, others tied them around their heads, or they used them as baby-slings to carry their children. In the 90s, young girls in the city rarely put them on, but a few did in the villages. I concluded that chitenje fabric was too old-fashioned, too outdated and too uncool for young girls who wanted to look like hip city kids—girls like me. In some ways, I wanted to be considered respectful and well-behaved, but I reflexively rebelled against Malawian customs and behaviors associated with good girls—those passive personalities that only attracted muted or subdued interactions with people. Malawian fashion and cooking were only two of many things I rebelled against. I became a phenomenon, a rare Malawian breed whom many tried to figure out. It even became common for people to ask me what, exactly, I was becoming: "What kind of girl refuses to wear a chitenje?" some would ask, shaking their heads. "What kind of girl doesn't want to cook?" others would inquire, followed by a cluck that emphasized how appalling I was. "What kind of girl behaves like this?" some would say, clapping their hands loudly, mouths agape as if they had just witnessed something unfathomable. But the question that struck me the most, the one that was often accompanied by the look of puzzlement on the faces of those who asked, was "What kind of girl are you?" This question made me feel most alien.

To those who encountered me, I was either an outgoing person or a rude brat with no morals or culture. The television actresses I watched became guides for my female identity. Angela Bassett, Phylicia Rashad, Halle Berry, Oprah Winfrey, Vanessa Williams—from their performances, I found strands of the kind of girl I wanted to be. They were always women who were significantly older than I was because they exhibited more power than young girls I met in both domestic and public spaces. Of course, the lives that were portrayed in American movies and sitcoms always looked more appealing, but it wasn't so much their glamour as the power they had. Their fictional lives overshadowed the life I lived in Malawi, where women were secondary to men and strangely expected to be small, coy, and fragile. *There is something I'm missing,* I always thought. Back then, I never thought that American women struggled with similar expectations. My focus was only on those powerful female characters. When other Malawians said "*Iwetu,* you're crazy. *Kodi* you think you are American?" I, indeed, gravitated to whatever I saw on American television, seeking expressions that would liberate me from passive personas. American women seemed freer on T.V.—free in fashion and in their own bodies. And the more I was drawn to how they walked with tall, confident, upright postures—chests out and chins held high—the more I was told the police would arrest me for behaving like a boy. When I copied how American women interacted with the opposite sex, speaking their minds without making themselves small, I was usually insulted about behaving nothing like a girl: "*Kamwa ngati mamuna,*" meaning "you have a mouth like a boy." *There is something wrong with me,* I always thought.

Even though they were just female characters on T.V., they seemed to have options to become any kind of person they chose, and I wanted those options, too. I started to refuse wearing chitenjes and, for comfort, wore jeans instead. Even as a pre-teen, I wanted to cut my hair short, like Halle Berry, but still be considered beautiful. I was sick of burning my scalp with chemical treatments that straightened my hair to look more like a *mzungu*, a white person. Instead of dolls, I wanted to play vigorous sports with boys because sports made me feel powerful.

I didn't understand Malawi. I felt caged in my country and felt its culture was something I had to break free from. The images I saw on American television sparked a desire to spread my wings, to find a wild song that sounded true to who I was. I was definitely a stubborn girl like my grandmother. Maybe I was the kind of girl my grandfather would reprimand and exorcize with his eyes, but I had guts like my worm-digging father, the tiny snake-survivor. Like him, I made so many curious choices as a child. I dared to dig up my own dreams and to find ways to survive other people's expectations. And when people disapproved of my behavior, when they demanded that I carry myself differently, at least I was the girl who could say "Oh, *hell* no!"

Haunted Girl

In the middle of the night, I awoke to a stampede outside my bedroom window. The room was dark, and my curtains were illuminated in yellow from whatever was happening outside. Silhouettes, bodies—too many of them. Running. I was confused. *Why are these people outside my window in the middle of the night?*

I knew there was evil. The kind that physically hurts people. The kind that kills. Not evil from made-up, imaginative tales but from the world I lived in. At six years old, the stories that frightened me most were about mysterious murders and witchcraft practices that my friends and cousins told me about; like the old man who was robbed one night on a dirt road that led to a dark cornfield near my house. His lifeless body was found twisted up amongst cornstalks, a huge gash on his head, blood spilling everywhere. Or the dismembered bodies that the police kept finding in junkyards. Rumor had it that, in Malawi, body parts were selling like hotcakes and being used for witchcraft rituals. One middle-aged man with a wife and two kids was advised by a witchdoctor that if he wanted to become rich or gain good fortune, he either had to steal people's organs for a powerful spell or engage in sexual acts with his mother or youngest daughter. Some say the wife was never in on this deal. And eventually, the police found hearts, livers, arms and legs hidden away in a refrigerator. I always prayed that nobody would do such a thing to my family. My parents tried to keep my mind free from disturbing things, especially fatal accidents—anything death-related. If we watched movies that happened to have violent killings or blood and gore, one of my brothers would cover my eyes until the scenes finished. If there were scenes with strange voodoo or satanic heads swiveling around like Linda Blair in *The Exorcist*, a movie I had once secretly watched without permission, I covered my own eyes (while peeking through my fingers).

*

We lived in Sunny Side, where painted brick houses had big lawns with perfectly cut green grass. A multitude of flowers complemented the vastness of the space, and giant metal gates rolled open to reveal yards resembling the exotic vacation spots you see in brochures or television ads. Before my parents could afford a house in Sunny Side, they had experienced being poor. As a boy, my father sold worms to fishermen. When he was about twelve years old, he attended Sir Robert Sinclair Primary School, and my grandfather paid for his tuition. At the time, my grandfather worked at the Imperial Tobacco Company in Limbe and my grandmother was a stay-at-home mom. Though my grandfather's job helped to make ends meet, he couldn't always afford my father's school fees. As a result, my father sold worms to European men who went fishing as a recreational activity at a place called Barn Dam. My father suspects it was named after one of the old British colonialists. African men were never found fishing for fun at the dam.

My father and his friends would run barefoot from school, still wearing their uniforms, khaki shorts and shirts, ready to dig along the Limbe river with their bare hands. Because the lawn was nicely cut, the constant fear of snakes was diminished, but catching a disease called bilharzia or "snail fever" was another story. The infection came from parasitic worms that live in fresh water. Symptoms include a rash, fever, body aches, and breathing difficulties. If the disease reaches a chronic stage, you can suffer from diarrhea, painful urination, and sometimes you can even find blood in the urine or feces. Luckily my father never caught such a disease. When he extracted the worms from the soil, he placed them in a can. The Europeans would either buy the whole can or ask my father and his friends to come along and put the worms on fishing rods as bait. The payment came when the job was done. After my father finished primary school, he went on to high school and passed his O-level Cambridge examinations, attaining his General Certificate of Secondary Education. For years, he wanted to pursue a business that would earn him more money to build an independent life. My father never went to college, but in 1971, he applied for a job at an insurance company. He started as a clerk, learning to understand what insurance was about. His favorite part was learning something new each day as he filed paperwork and wrote different kinds of insurance policies. As he worked his way up, he became the most traveled man in the company, visiting places like the United Kingdom, Switzerland, Germany and India; because of all the knowledge he gained in insurance, most of his colleagues wanted to be taught by him. Everyone wanted to be mentored by Montfort Ben Kautsire. It was no surprise that after many years of hard work, my father eventually landed a manager position.

My mother was a florist. She, too, began with very little. In education, she only went as far as high school, always scoring at the top of her class. For a while, she worked as a cashier at People's Trading Center (P.T.C.), which was like Malawi's version of an American Stop and Shop. Later, she applied for a position as an airhostess for Malawi Airways, traveling the world just like my father. Before my mother owned her flower business, she grew about twenty to thirty plants, which she sold on her front porch. At the time, people didn't appreciate the beauty and significance of plants. It was a miracle if she got a customer. Many people teased and mocked her about her plant business—strangers, friends, and even family. When she waited for customers, people asked her condescending questions, the tone of their voices emphasizing how plants were useless, unwanted things.

"Lilian, why waste time with flowers?"

"Lilian, why not open a restaurant instead? At least with food, people eat every day. But flowers? Who eats flowers?"

Yet my mother persisted, usually muting all the negative voices as she sat on the floor of our front porch, carefully watering and trimming her plants. She treated them as if they were her children, cleaning their thick green leaves to a healthy shine, organizing them in neat rows in

28

patterns only she knew would make the house look immaculate. My mother was content with plants. Her love for them was undeniable, and with this love, people caught on to how beautiful a home can look when plants are tended to with care. Like my father, years later, her business grew. With over thirty people working for her, she won landscaping contracts, decorating and maintaining the premises of big companies. She even named her company after herself: "Lily of the Valley."

When my father built the Sunny Side house in the early 90s, he was thinking of his future retirement. A big white, three-bedroom, brick-house with a red roof, a garage in the front yard and three terraces in the backyard with green grass, trees, plants, vegetables, and fruits. Construction lasted ten months. We would always have a home which he built on his own, he said—a comfortable home in a good neighborhood. In Malawi, we became an upper-class family that could also afford to hire cooks, guards, and gardeners. My parents believed in providing jobs for those who were less fortunate because they always remembered their own humble beginnings.

My father often checked the locks to every door that led into the house, whether it was day or night. I saw him casually circling the yard on a sunny afternoon, taking puffs of his favorite cigarette brand, Benson and Hedges, special filter. As he strolled around the house, he gave each door he passed a quick nudge to make sure.

"Where is the key for this door?" he would shout to one of the garden boys, seeking an answer that would reassure him that the keys were in a safe place, that random people did not have access to his home.

Other times, he noticed muddy handprints on the white walls of the house, which he always suspected were the workings of me and my "little friends."

"Ms. Kautsire!" he would summon me, "Why are you writing on my house with your dirty fingers?" He addressed me by my last name when he wanted to show that he took me seriously or when he held me accountable for something.

I would find him analyzing the handprints, standing in his Pierre Cardin suit, the arm with a cigarette folded around his belly and the other stroking his chin as if he were in deep thought. His usual stoic, Sydney Poitier demeanor. I would stand before him, then, guilty, like a fragile little creature with big, round eyes.

"It wasn't me," I would lie, "*Mwina* it was Charles or Trevor." Though he knew my brothers never played with mud.

"Do not touch my walls with your dirty hands, Ms. Kautsire," he would say with a serious face, wagging his finger at me. Then, he would smile as he turned to continue circling the house, his way of playfully communicating that he knew I had been caught in a lie.

The garden and indoor decorations were tended to meticulously. Even my mother walked around the house in her chitenje, removing weeds that grew among the flowers and the grass. She plucked the plants from her nursery and made flower arrangements, which she placed in different rooms of the house. Some were made from driftwood and artificial plants. Sometimes, she taught me how to design them. I learned how to pierce flowers through sponges that were glued at the center of driftwoods. If my piercing-strategy was good, if I carefully contrasted the colors of the flowers, I created the most beautiful arrangements. My parents liked everything to be neat. Organized. Well-ordered. We believed that Sunny Side was a safe neighborhood. The brick-houses belonged to middle and upper-class families, and if their yards did not already have a brick fence with electricity charged barbwire at the top, they had fences made from thick straw, neatly patched together to surround the house. Ours was made from straw. For the most part, we *were* safe and undisturbed by others (aside from my naughty friend, Mavuto, who stole mangoes from our backyard tree that draped into her yard). But the 90s were a time when poverty had struck Malawi fiercely. Houses were getting broken into. People were getting desperate for food and money. Houses belonging to middle and upper-class families became targets for theft, fences or no fences. There was no such thing as a safe neighborhood.

*

Two years after our move to Sunny Side, our neighborhood became notorious for burglaries. We heard stories about thieves tying up and stabbing people in their own homes or threatening to microwave newborn babies if families did not cooperate with their demands. I was glad that I was not a newborn baby. Two blocks away from our house, a whole family was killed by a gang of thieves. Their house was set on fire, and later, the guard gave a police report of how he escaped by jumping over the fence as he heard things exploding inside the house. It was no longer safe to walk around the neighborhood after 6 PM. Thieves hid under patches of leaves or in cornfields, waiting to rob their next victim. We were horrified, making sure that every door in the house was locked at night. With so many houses around us being robbed, my father immediately hired two guards. Security alarms were also installed. My father explained our safety plan. If thieves showed up, the guards would blow their whistles to notify us of the danger outside the house. We would press the security alarm, which sent a signal for help from the National Guard Security, a team of men in pickup trucks who drove around Sunny Side, ready to chase thieves away. Then, we would pray. Having this system in place made my family feel safer. We continued to sleep in peace, our faith in the hands of God, and our night guards.

I usually had good dreams. Darkness didn't scare me. I slept alone in a single bed with pink covers, soft pillows, in *My Little Pony* pajamas. No night light needed—I was a big girl. My dreams often involved flying with cats and dogs or visiting magical lands made of cookies, candy and other edible sugary things, like the witch's house in *Hansel and Gretel*. My mind was quick to merge children's books and television with the real world. Even when I was awake, my imagination remained at work. Sometimes, I was a Power Ranger morphing into my superhero outfit to administer some serious butt-kicking; other times, one of the Powerpuff Girls, filled with "sugar, spice, and everything nice," pretending that the dangerous chemical X in my bloodstream was sending me to the ground with sudden convulsions, slowly gaining superpowers that would allow me to leap back up and take down imaginary villains. I would shoot monsters, zap witches with my own magic wands, toss grenades at mad scientists and run for cover behind living room sofas. My parents were the audience to my butt-kicking sessions in our living-room, proud to have their "Sweet Caroline" so keen to restore peace in the world.

If I was not busy being a superhero, I was Dee Dee from *Dexter's Laboratory*, trying to find ways to hang out with my two older brothers. Both were teenagers, thirteen and eighteen, too cool to play with their six-year-old sister. They saw me as a constant annoyance, yelling at me to get out of their room, to stop going through their stuff. But I just wanted to convince them I was "cool" too. When Charles, the middle child, was not home, I played his Super Nintendo. I spent hours mastering Super Mario, making it through advanced levels of the game, excited to show him how skilled I was. There were always two outcomes: either he was impressed that I finished a level he was stuck on, or he was angry—not only for playing his video game without permission but for completing levels he could not.

Trevor, meanwhile, was my role model. I wanted to carry myself the way he did, so I often snuck into his wardrobe and wore his baggy clothes. It was filled with the latest designs—Adidas t-shirts, FUBU jeans, Nike caps, and Reebok headbands. I even accessorized with his sunglasses, bandanas and gold chains. If it were possible, I would have put on everything at once. Then, I ran around the house in his clothes, mimicking his mannerisms: throwing peace signs at people while screaming "Yo! Yo! Yo!"; frequently grabbing my crotch the way he did, like Michael Jackson; stroking my mouth and chin if I wanted to say something fresh like "Wassup, homie!" or "What's poppin', player!" I would be a "smooth brotha" like Trevor said he was. *Who wouldn't want to be around me?* I thought. A clever, cool, butt-kicking superhero. I felt like I could save my family if the world were under attack. I would hide them under my bed until whatever was after us had passed, lovingly shush their whispers. "It's okay," I would say, "I'll keep you safe." I would be their protector.

*

The stampede outside my bedroom window grew louder. I sat up in bed and rubbed the sleep from my eyes. The silhouettes were multiplying. *Do we have unexpected guests?* There was no clock in my room for me to tell how long I had been asleep, if the night was still young enough for visitors to be welcomed. I looked at the corner of my room to see if any light was seeping through the top and bottom spaces of the door, in case my parents or brothers were still up, but everything was dark. I began to slip out of bed to go find my parents, but then I heard a booming male voice speaking Chichewa outside my window.

"You will suffer today! *Simunati!* We are not done with you yet!"

My heart pounded. I felt like it was ready to pop out of my chest. *Do they mean me? Who is YOU?* I took deep breaths to contain the fear taking over me. One leg stuck out of my blanket, shaking with hesitation as I decided whether to stay in bed and hide or run towards my bedroom door to seek my family.

Door-hacking. Glass-smashing. This was what I heard. Our living room had two side-doors. One door was near the backyard and the other in the front, adjacent to my room. If you entered the house through the front living room door and walked five steps in, there was a hallway on the left, which led to our bedrooms. My room was on the left side of the hall, facing the front yard, where all the commotion was taking place, and my brothers' and parents' room on the right, facing the backyard. The living room side-doors were made of glass that had small wires inside of it, framed with thick, brown wood. The door adjacent to my bedroom window was the first one I heard smashed. I knew our hardwood kitchen door was just a few feet past the glass side-door, and it was being chopped to pieces. By an ax? A machete? Were they men in dark clothes, masked bandits, swinging and poking at the doors with rusty metal rods? I didn't know. Whatever weapons these were, they meant doom for my family. They would use them to kill us. I began to cry while forcing myself out of bed. Blood rushed through my veins like a monstrous current, creating an unbearable tingling sensation under my skin. Sweat formed around my forehead. My palms were clammy, but my neck was surprisingly cold. Standing still felt uncomfortable, as if being motionless would make the thieves detect where I was. I paced around my small square room. The hacking noises grew louder, and I heard vicious ripping and desperate dismantling. My imagination ran wild: picturing thieves kicking in the doors, others tearing off dangling pieces of glass and wood to make a wider entry way. I imagined bodies bending down to fit themselves into giant, gaping holes in the doors. I shook off the images, then looked at my window. Silhouettes were still flashing past.

"*Msanga! Msanga!*" someone shouted, commanding everyone to hurry up.

Every shadow, every footstep, every crack or crash created a terror in me I had never felt before. I paced around, unable to touch anything. My steps felt heavy and my body was on the verge of collapse. I cried as silently as I could manage, muffling loud sobs, taking deep breaths, trying to hold myself together. I knew not to scream for help because that would only invite thieves to come directly at me. This was a new kind of evil, but it was nothing like what I had imagined in my childish fantastical worlds. This evil was paralyzing. It was merciless. It was real. And it had finally found its way into my life.

Outside, the hacking had ceased. The danger was now inside the house. Then the whistles went off. I stood still for a second. I knew wherever the guards were, they were running for their lives. Their whistles sounded from different parts of our yard. I would later learn that the guards had been hiding in the darkness of the gardens, struggling to do their job—to warn us.

Danger is disorienting. My mind veered into unusual patterns of thought at a time of crisis. Hearing all the breaking glass made me think of how the doors once stood intact. For a brief moment, I thought of how disappointed my parents would be when they saw the destruction happening to their home, to all the expensive things—the television, stereo, glass tables, glass doors. The disappointment on their faces. How meaningless everything must have seemed to thieves. I pictured them running off without any care, no thought for what it took to build a house, to keep a beautiful home or for the people whose lives they would change forever with a frightening attack.

Then questions spun. *Are my parents and brothers hearing this? How could anyone sleep through all the noise?* I wondered why no one was coming to my room to get me. I thought of my father, over-protective, a man so concerned about my well-being, a man who would become so furious with the whole family if I didn't eat supper. *Where was he?* I thought about my mother, warm and affectionate, the way we snuggled when we watched television, my tiny body wiggling next to her side for comfort. She defended me from my brothers whenever they chased me around to give me a whooping for going through their stuff. Hiding behind her body was like hiding behind Captain America's shield, the protection felt bulletproof. Indestructible.

Where was she tonight?

Where were my brothers?

I began to weigh scenarios of *why* they were not coming. Maybe they weren't awake because most of the commotion was on the front side of the house, near my room, and their rooms faced the backyard. Sometimes they slept with the television turned on loud. Maybe the noise was muffled and the sound waves did not reach their rooms. Maybe they were deep-sleepers.

Alone. I crouched at the corner of the room, right above my window. I did not want to look at the silhouettes anymore or hear the banging and crashing that wouldn't stop. The sounds were all I could use to decipher how terribly they were wrecking the house. Things were being pushed around, cupboards and drawers were being opened and slammed. Sometimes it sounded like everything was being torn down from walls and ledges, and other times I didn't know what the object was but it sounded like thunder when it's right over the house. I wanted to pray to God, but I struggled to find the words. My parents were Catholic and they had told me that God was good at saving people, like a superhero. I always worried that I had never met him in person, but I believed in him just like I believed in all the other heroes from books and cartoons. *Please, God, make them go away. I hope you can hear me.*

No one was coming to rescue us. Time was passing by and no one in my family was coming to protect me. I flashed on a reality where we were all killed, our bodies lying limp on the floor, the walls of the room splattered with our blood. I couldn't bear to think of the loss, the horror, or what it might feel like to die. I had to do something. I thought of what my father would do, remembering his advice after the alarms were installed. "No matter what happens during a robbery, our goal should be to press that alarm. Then the police will come." There were two buttons in the house; one was in my parents' bedroom and the other was in the corridor that ran from our bedrooms to the living room. I worried that my parents hadn't pressed theirs yet. I worried that no one was coming to help us. *Be brave like a superhero. Go into the corridor and press the security alarm.*

They were banging the door in the corridor.

"*Tatsegulani*!" a voice demanded that we open it.

I could feel my heart beating very loudly as I took small hesitant steps towards my bedroom door, like a child learning how to walk. I reached for the knob and slowly opened the door. More darkness. The corridor was empty. I looked to my brothers' bedroom across the hallway, then to the left at my parents' room. Their doors were closed. I looked to the right, where the corridor connects to the living room. The door at the end was shaking from loud banging. *I hope they don't start chopping it down.* I was trembling so much that I could have tripped over my own feet from unsteady walking. I could hear sofas being dragged on the floor, fragile cabinet displays thrown around recklessly, voices giving orders to hurry up and pack things. And the alarm button was right next to the wooden door—the door that led to danger.

As I drew near it, the thieves hacked deeper into the wood. I flinched at the first hack. My body tightened. I was aware that at any minute, it would burst open and I would be the next thing to take the ax. But something inside me gave me the guts to keep walking, to keep seeing myself press the button. Each loud bang shook my heart. Each loud bang was like an invisible blow in the face and, at times, I paused and failed to lift my leg to take the next step. What would I say to them if they broke it down? Would I even have time to say anything or would I have a spear lodged in my chest before I could utter the words, "Please don't hurt me."

But *there* was the alarm, tucked in the corner of the wall adjacent to the trembling door. The sight of it gave me hope. Because I was very short, I stood on my tiptoes as my fingers fidgeted against the wall, reaching for the press. No luck. I began to leap up and down, slamming my tiny body against the wall several times. With the loud banging on the door next to me, I became more and more desperate with my leaps. I knew it was a matter of life and death. So, I leapt. And leapt. And leapt. And leapt. Until, for one split second, I felt my index finger push the button in—success.

A door flew open. My brothers ran into the corridor, and before I could say a word, Trevor scooped me up from the ground and carried me back into my room.

"What the hell are you doing in the corridor?" he whispered loudly. He wouldn't stop pacing. Charles too. Their eyes were wide open, fear-stricken. I suspected they had just woken up. There was no time to explain about the alarm, and I was only grateful someone had finally come to protect me. Charles rushed to my window and knelt down. As both my brothers peeked through the curtains, I hid under the bed to avoid triggering more panic. It was safer not to look. But more thoughts took over:

What are we going to do?

Wondering if security would make it to our house before the thieves hurt us.

Did the alarm work?

Wondering why my parents still weren't coming out of their room.

Did the thieves already get to them? Are they still alive?

Wondering if this will be the night we would all die.

I don't want to die.

My mind had memorized the sounds of hacking and smashing, and my imagination ran wild again—visualizing axes and machetes cutting through our bodies. In my mind, these thieves were already making us bleed because we owned things, because we dared to have a good home. Maybe they saw us as monsters, rich people they needed to humble through fear. Maybe they saw greedy people who prevented *them* from owning what was in *our* house. I remembered, again, the torture tactics I had heard about. Our family had no baby for thieves to microwave. So would I be the bait to get my parents to do as the thieves demanded? What if someone wanted to chop off my fingers? Since they were shouting threats outside my window, I envisioned them as villains who wanted to boast about harming us. Thieves were known to make strange requests, and I feared they might want us to witness each other suffer if we did not do what they asked. I couldn't bear the thought of my mother, the kindest and gentlest woman I knew, being tortured. I would demand the thieves to kill me instead, if sacrifices count. Maybe it would be better to die first so I wouldn't have to watch my family suffer. I kept weighing different ways to die. My heart hurt. As I lay under the bed with my brothers, fear and darkness reached for my core. I trembled while my mind created nightmares, nightmares that would haunt me for years. The cracking noises. The shadows. These thieves.

*

New sounds swarmed the house: car sirens, dog barks, police whistles, and men shouting, "*Akuba*!" "Thieves!" My brothers and I looked at the shadows on the curtains. More running. Flashing silhouettes. But this time they were running in different directions. Some even stopped right by my window, which made me hold my breath, hoping they weren't about to smash the glass, but they moved on. Maybe that was God intervening. There was less banging and crashing in the living room. Then I heard a door unlock in the corridor. A familiar sound. Two clicks and a chain-lock.

My parents' bedroom door. (The chain-lock was to prevent workers from stealing money or other valuable things they kept in their room). My brothers and I walked into the corridor with unsure steps. I held Trevor's hand tightly. We saw my father first. He walked out in his cotton, blue and brown striped robe, eyes distant as if he had seen a ghost. I rushed to hug his side, my tiny arms stretched around his waist, squeezing him as hard as possible. My brothers walked behind us with my mother. Her arms wrapped around her body as if she was protecting herself from something.

"It's okay now. They are gone. Security is here now," my father said. A guard had knocked on my parents' window to notify them that the coast was clear. That's also when I learned that my parents had only woken up during the last moments of the robbery. Their television was on, and both my parents were used to the sound of loud noises from action movies. Only this time, the noises were inside their house. When they woke up, the security guards were chasing away the thieves. Help had already arrived. We walked towards the door that led to the living room. When my father opened it, there were large cracks on the other side of the door. I was surprised it was still standing.

Even as we passed through the corridor door, I feared that some of the thieves might still be inside the house. They had become invisible phantoms, appearing and disappearing in corners of our house. There was no sound of moving people, but the sight was a horrific mess. The glass doors that led to the living room were completely shattered. One was unhinged, and all that was left was an opening with no door. Most of the furniture was gone. The room was so empty that people could hear the echo of their own voices as they spoke. I was not speaking. I could not stop shaking, and I could not leave my father's side, fearing that if we separated, a lingering thief might grab me. I could hear my mother rummaging through the kitchen drawers. Maybe she wanted to see the horror of how much was taken, or maybe she wanted to see what was left. I also feared that thieves might still be in the kitchen. Someone might leap out of a corner and threaten to kill my mother. And who knew if other thieves were still hiding in our garden. I now hated that we had a big yard. At night, it became a garden of evil where danger could lurk. Each time my father looked at me, I could see the fury in his bloodshot eyes. He surely could see the fear in mine. My body felt stiff—hands held together, fingers intertwined, folded tightly on my chest. I could have cried at any second. I tugged at my father's robe. He looked down, holding me close to him.

"Daddy, I pressed the alarm!" I had always called him "dad," but on this night, fear had made a tough six-year-old girl so vulnerable that, without even thinking, the word, "daddy," sprung out instead. At that moment, I needed my father to be my protector. He smiled, rubbing my shoulder. I collapsed into his side.

"Good, Ms. Kautsire! You saved us," he said.

I looked around the living room to see if my brothers were nearby. I wished they could have heard my father acknowledge that I had saved the family, that I was the brains behind the rescue. As the police looked around the house, I heard my father making demands for them to do everything in their power to catch the thieves. He took one officer aside and began to describe his plan of action. He wanted to build a tall brick fence. He wanted to hire two more guards. He wanted more security alarm buttons. He wanted to install burglar bars all around the house.

"...because my daughter needs to be able to sleep at night!" he shouted, his voice piping with desperation, his eyes tinged with disappointment. Whenever he caught me looking at his frustrated face, he controlled his own panic, trying to reassure me that everything would be okay. I knew he just wanted me to feel safe. But for many months after, I could not sleep alone in my room. I was even afraid to dream. A bed was prepared for me in my parents' bedroom. Each night, as I lay in bed in their room, it took me a long time to fall asleep. I hallucinated, saw shadows standing in the corners of the room with axes and machetes or silhouettes of bodies running past my parents' bedroom window. I listened to the sounds of the night, fearing that thieves might be back to destroy our home.

*

The thieves were caught. A week and a half had passed since our house got broken into and we found out that there were over fifty thieves in our yard on the night of the robbery. *That mob could have killed my family.* The thought made my stomach queasy. It made me detest having a big house. *If we had a smaller house, we wouldn't have to worry about getting robbed*, I thought. *Why did my father buy this house? And why did God let him buy it if he knew we would be in danger?* I didn't know what kind of superhero God was, but I remember thinking if he was meant to be all-knowing, then our robbery proved otherwise. He would have known that our house was an attraction for danger. Maybe I should have been more grateful that he saved us that night. Maybe he got caught up on blessing us with a home, a big expensive house. But that was not what I wanted. I didn't care for a big expensive house. I wanted a safe home.

My mother gave us details of what happened in court. Most of the thieves came from the village of Kampala, a rural area bordering Sunny Side. One of them was followed home by the police.

"They found his wife using our curtains as bed covers," my mother explained, "I thought the thieves would be grown men, but when I saw them in court, most of them were tiny, tiny, tiny boys! They looked like teenagers!"

First, I was shocked that they were young. Where were their parents? Who had convinced them to rob us? I wanted to know why. I wanted to know how they justified their burglary. While my mother expressed how it was a shame that they used curtains for sheets, I was confused about why she was feeling sad for people who had robbed us. Yet, I will admit that I had sympathy I didn't want to feel at the time. I imagined a thief arriving at his home, excited to give his wife our curtains. "Lay this on our bed!" he would say to her. She would do it gracefully, thanking God that her husband could afford them, without any idea that he had stolen them. Or maybe she would know, but having bed covers would be better than freezing at night. Then I imagined an officer arriving in his car. Barging into the house. Searching. Finding our curtains on their bed. The wife, gripping her head-wrap in shock, her chitenje

45

dropping from her waist, weeping as another officer handcuffs her husband.

Another thief, who was a bit older than the rest, demanded that the trial be held in English (rather than Chichewa) because he was a graduate from the college of Polytechnic. My mother said he was trying to appear intelligent. I pictured him as a ringleader, using his wisdom to plan destruction. He would give a speech to the younger thieves, emphasizing ideals similar to Robin Hood's famous premise—steal from the rich and give to the poor. Only *they* would be stealing for themselves. The younger thieves would cheer at their college-educated leader, certain that his philosophy justified their robbery. Or maybe none of this happened. Maybe they were just following illegal methods of acquiring wealth, twisted strategies of thievery that were becoming prominent, slowly evolving into Malawian norms. It had never occurred to me that those who robbed houses at night would be educated. Intelligence did not cancel out poverty, and whether someone lived in a poor village or rich town, they were still capable of burglary. When people are faced with poverty, they become desperate to make ends meet, to feed their families. They may risk their lives, their futures—harming others, destroying homes, becoming someone's worst nightmare. And educated people are not exempt from this.

Some of the fifty-plus thieves were locked in jail, I was told. This made my family feel better. There was some form of justice. For the next few months, a tall brick fence was built around our house. We now had four nightshift guards, more security alarms, and burglar bars. The guards could also press the alarms from the outside since they were the

46

first to spot danger. Many neighborhoods implemented a night-watch system where a group of men, dressed as ninjas, walked around with giant knives. Every few hours, they sharpened their weapons in the streets to scare any thieves that might want to ambush people. This ninja strategy lessened some of the neighborhood attacks and it helped guards during their night watch. The Sunny Side robbery was my first near-death experience, and, although at age six, I still had many good dreams that colored the worlds I visited in my sleep, the darkness from the burglary became deeply rooted inside me. Massive mobs. Hacking. Smashing. Trembling doors. Whistles. Our home was under constant attack in recurring dreams, and I was always trying to be the hero who saves my family. Even today, in my adult life, my subconscious still conjures nightmare robberies. They manifest, again, the sounds, shadows, thieves who never stop haunting me—no matter where I live.

Ngoni Girl

*

Before I would allow myself to behave like a child, I wanted to be an adult. I wanted the power and knowledge that came with being big. Childhood felt like a curse I couldn't outgrow fast enough. And before I had reached an age where I could discover for myself the empowering aspects of being female, I struggled with understanding the ideals established for young girls. My instincts gravitated towards emulating what I thought was adulthood. I mimicked the things I heard men and women do or say—tone of voice, humor, sarcasm, body language—anything that was different from a child. Then, I set out to do things that were just not meant for children. This became apparent when I started drinking alcohol. More specifically, the first time I ever got drunk. I was eight years old.

*

Half a can of beer was coursing through my eight-year-old body. I felt like I had discovered the essence of life. Seated alone in my Aunt Lonia's living room on a cream-colored sofa, I sipped on a can of beer. Castle Lager. My face felt flushed, and my body was strangely warm and light. I had developed a taste for beer because each time Aunt Lonia, my father's sister, poured it, I asked to drink the foam at the top of the glass. It looked like a milkshake, which probably influenced my fondness for such a bitter-tasting drink. Enjoying the bitterness meant being an adult. My Aunt Lonia was a big woman with dark eyes and a wide and gracious smile which revealed the gap between her two front teeth. She had a loud, booming voice and laughed easily at anything. Each time I visited her house, I found her wearing an apron over her clothes because she spent a lot of time preparing food in the kitchen for every guest she received. Usually relatives. Her favorite light dish was fried chicken or beef with a salad on the side. She called this *khwasu khwasu*, which implies how someone devours food. These light dishes were always served with alcohol, something that my Ngoni tribe relatives appreciated.

In the Ngoni tribe, it wasn't a terrible thing if children tasted alcohol. The origins of our ethnic group traced back to the famously strong Zulu people of South Africa. We were descendants of the legendary African warrior, King Shaka Zulu, and a King's children had to be strong. Even my last name, Kautsire, means "go and pour" because my great-grandfather on my father's side used to be a cupbearer for a Ngoni tribe. If the chief became thirsty for water or alcohol, he would yell, "Kautsire!" to which my great-grandfather would then rush to do as requested. In fact, I had heard my aunts and uncles say if a child could handle their liquor then it meant they were tough. I started believing this, and I wanted to be tough. When Aunt Lonia allowed me to sip the foam, I snuck in a huge gulp of beer and told her it was an accident. She knew I was lying.

Sometimes she jokingly wagged a finger at me and prophesied that I would grow up to be a beer-loving girl.

"No way!" I shouted, fearing her assumption would not only put me on a list of bad girls, but sinners who would burn in hell. My family was Catholic, and I was warned by Christian friends that hell was not a place I wanted to end up in. "I'm a good girl, auntie!" I shouted desperately, sulking as if I was on the verge of crying. Then I modified my lie. "The liquid is too bitter for me, yuck! But the foam is okay," like some kind of eight-year-old beer connoisseur. My parents were fine with the beer-foam sipping, but they never encouraged drinking alcohol, often warning me and my brothers about the dangers of drinking. They explained the misfortunes and bad choices people made when they got drunk—car accidents, unwanted pregnancies, police arrests after someone's rowdy behavior. For the most part, my brothers and I stuck with the sipping and stayed clear from drinking large amounts of alcohol. Yet sometimes, being a nosey child, I hid in the corners of our living room, eavesdropping on the conversations my father had with his friends, while they drank Carlsberg beers and ate boiled pig feet (food that was famous among drinkers). They talked about what Ngoni men found satisfying in life. I even picked up one statement they often repeated: "All that a Ngoni man needs is his wife, his meat and his drink." Then, they would laugh in agreement. It was probably okay for my father to enjoy an adult conversation with his friends, and maybe what they said was true for some Ngoni men. But at eight years old, I failed to understand that what they were saying did not apply to me. Instead, I took it as an ideal, disregarding the fact that they were grown men and I was just a little girl.

When I stole the can of Castle Lager from Aunt Lonia's refrigerator, I was convinced that I was ready to promote myself from being a skilled beer-sipping con artist to an official drinker of an entire can of beer. Aunt Lonia was showering in her bedroom, and I intended to finish the can before she came to check on me. I had been chugging it for less than ten minutes when I stood up from the sofa to go and pee. The room began to spin. I sat back down instantly, then laid my head on a cushion. *So this is what it means to be drunk.* I had seen drunk people before, both awake and passed out. They were either happy, sad, or mean drunks. I wanted the effects of a happy drunk because the looseness of their speech and body language looked like fun. They also laughed a lot and danced more freely. They seemed to have more courage to do silly things, too. I closed my eyes, hoping the spinning would cease. Then I thought of the can I was holding, fearing that my aunt would catch me indulging in alcohol. I jumped up very quickly and rushed to the kitchen. Everything was moving—walls, doors, kitchen cabinets, chairs and tables, the fridge, the floor. I buried the beer-can in the trash by the kitchen sink, making sure I covered it with other things that were thrown away. Then I ran back to the living room to lay down on the couch. My heart raced unusually fast, and my body was heating up. I wondered how drunk I was, and if I was going to pass out or hurl. I hated throwing up because it happened to me each time I suffered from malaria. I hated how I couldn't control things coming out of me, the uncomfortable feeling of strange fluids flowing through my throat. It frightened me.

Drunkenness felt like I had malaria. I closed my eyes again and hoped it would stop. I prayed. "Please God, help me. I'll never drink again. I promise to be a very good girl." Then, I waited for God to come through.

I never threw up. The prayer was answered. God had allowed me to fall asleep that afternoon, and Aunt Lonia never experienced the horror of discovering a drunk eight-year-old niece. She didn't even ask why I had fallen asleep in the middle of the day, something she had never seen me do. God had covered all the troubling bases. When I woke up, I was sober but drained. I said nothing about how I felt. And like anyone hurting from a hangover, I vowed to never drink again. It was a sincere vow. I even believed that I could keep my promise to God—to be a very good girl.

Tough Skin

The door flew open, causing a thunderous bang. I began to shake under my pink bedcovers, caught in the middle of an attempt to escape my cooking chore. Someone was standing in my room. "*Tadzuka pamenepo*! In the kitchen! Now!" It was my mother's voice, in a tone that was no longer soft and deep. There were sharp blades in her shriek. I slowly lowered my blanket from my head, frowning like a wounded puppy. Her arm was stretched out, holding the door open. Her face looked flushed, head tilted to the side, eyes wide open, mouth slightly agape with shock—disbelief in my behavior. Back then, I saw my mother as a woman with two extreme temperaments. On the one hand, she was a soft-spoken, gentle woman who wouldn't hurt a fly, and on the other, she could flare up with hot words and put anybody in their place like Tyler Perry's Madea. My mother's rage was always palpable. Her growing fury would make you see glowing fires in her eyes. I sulked some more, continuing to lay in bed, wishing the whole house would collapse into the ground because of the kitchen battle ahead. Maybe if I rebelled longer, she would leave me alone.

"I said *now!*" she yelled, dropping her arm from the door.

My body shot up as if I had been laying on a trampoline. I stood beside my bed, straightening my t-shirt, adjusting my jeans, hoping she would move from the doorway. My parents never hit me, but the combination of her agitated shriek and stern face had scared me enough to pause and prepare for a possible beating. She clucked, then stormed towards the kitchen. I followed.

Hot *ufa* porridge bubbled in a big silver pot on our white stove. My mother had covered it with a lid. I was familiar with the trembling action inside the pot. We were cooking *nsima*, a staple food in Malawi. The steps to prepare it sound simple. After allowing the porridge to boil for about five minutes, you add more maize flour (the *ufa*) and stir until it reaches a dough-like state. Then, you scoop it onto a plate with a wooden spoon, and enjoy it with a *ndiwo* of your choice—vegetables, chicken, beef or fish stew.

"Finish cooking this nsima," she said, pointing at the pot.

The lid made bubbling noises. I clucked, then glanced at the kitchen door that led outside with the look of someone ready to run away. My mother was still pointing at the pot, searching my face, as if she was waiting for a remark that would worsen her annoyance with my refusal to cook. I walked to the sink, eyes down, and washed my hands. My mother stood next to the stove, watching me pick the wooden stir-stick she had placed beside the pot. I planted my legs firmly onto the ground like the form of a runner at the start line of a race. My mind was filled with dread at the lake of fire beneath the lid. I held my breath, then with a sudden swift tug, lifted the cover and quickly jumped back. Hot blobs of porridge shot up; steam piped from the pot. The war had begun.

"So, *ukuchita chani*? What are you running away from?" my mother asked. She laughed a little, knowing exactly why I had jumped back.

I ignored her, placing the lid on the side of the stove, watching the steamy globs of porridge rage in the air. They exploded everywhere—stove, counter, and floor. My mother chuckled again, coarse throaty chuckles like villainous women I had seen on T.V., the ones who reveled in their evil plans. She pulled a chair and sat beside the wooden rectangular table at the center of the kitchen, folding her arms to watch me closely. I could see that my hesitation entertained her. All she was missing was a bucket of popcorn. This was my mother's technique, her way of teaching me how to cook without her intervention. I began to study the movement of the exploding blobs, how frequently they flew up, how far they shot in different directions, and I even listened for rhythms, recurring patterns in the splashing. Maybe if I mastered the motion, I could prevent the globs of fire from landing on my skin.

I drew closer, then scooped some ufa with a small plate. I poured it in the pot. I began to stir. The bubbles grew vicious, angered by the disruption of the ufa I had poured. I stirred faster, hoping the circling of the wooden stick would suppress some of the bubbling. Sweat formed around my forehead. I hunched my shoulders and squinted my eyes, fearing some blobs would splatter on my face. Then I poured and stirred, poured and stirred. Sometimes my scoops of ufa were so small that I tossed them from afar.

You would think I was throwing water into a pot to put out a fire. Ufa landed on the floor, some on the stove. Smoke rose from the hot coils.

"Ah-Ah!" my mother yelled, rising from her chair, "What are you doing? Don't you know how to cook nsima?" She shook her head. I saw the mysterious flames in her eyes. Yet, sometimes, I swear I could see a slight smirk at the corner of her mouth, as if she was holding back some much-needed laughter. But laughing at this moment would only demote her from her military rank of Lieutenant Mother in the kitchen wars. "Stand up straight and stir properly!" she sat back down.

I straightened my body. The nsima was getting firmer. Less bubbly. I moved closer to the stove, and just when I had carefully poured a large scoop of ufa in the pot, I noticed a thick layer of porridge making an up-and-down motion, like it was breathing. Then, I realized that it wasn't thick enough to suppress a hot blob that came flying onto my right arm. I screamed, dropping the wooden stir-stick, backing away from the stove. I held my scalded right arm with my left, and I was breathing deeply, panic written all over my face. I scanned my skin for the blisters I detested and moaned even if I didn't find any bumps.

"*Zoona*, Carol! Really?" my mother shouted, rising from her chair again. "Girls don't cook like this. Why are you so scared of a little burn?"

"Ma, it hurts," I whined, blowing cool breath on my upper right wrist.

"Let me see," she said, holding my arm gently. She examined my skin, searching for redness, moving my arm around carefully as if I had broken it. "*Oh pepa, sorry,*" she

56

said, elongating the sound of vowels in her words as if she was singing a song, blowing on my upper right wrist. Her voice was suddenly caring, sweet-sounding. To indulge in her spontaneous wave of concern, I made sobbing noises (no tears) just to signal how poorly I had been treated, to emphasize the traumatic horror her daughter had just suffered. As she examined my hand, I analyzed the reaction on her face, hoping the soft-spoken, gentle mother would reemerge to save me. My mother was skilled, fluent at performing a one-woman show of good-cop, bad-cop. She picked the wooden stir-stick from the floor and rinsed it at the sink. "You need to develop tough skin," she said, "I've been burnt many times, and now I'm used to it." True. The woman had fireproof skin. Several times I had watched her face when she was burned by the same steaming lumps; she would wince, then casually wipe the splatter from her hand and continue cooking. A blister would form but it healed in a day unless she willingly popped it.

My mother had made it clear—if I ever moved out of my parents' house, if I ever moved to America as I had always dreamed, I needed to know how to cook. If I ever got married, no husband would stay with a woman who didn't know how to cook. I often imagined that the terror of cooking would end if I moved to America. It was the television ads I had seen for kitchen appliances. Automatic this, automatic that, cooking looked simpler. In Malawi, we did everything by hand. We peeled potatoes with knives, de-veined the stems of *mkhwani* (pumpkin leaves), popped peas from their covers, picked rocks from rice, boiled water for tea and coffee. It was a bore to wait for bubbles. America would be my escape.

But sometimes I caught myself thinking differently about my hatred for cooking. My mother had anointed her lessons with questions that challenged me to rethink the pain and suffering in my kitchen wars: "What kind of girl screams from little nsima burns? What kind of girl doesn't know how to cut a whole chicken? What kind of girl doesn't want to cook?" The questions advertised the possibility of being a normal girl. They were invitations, beckoning me to accomplish what they asked. The more my mother used them, the more I rewired my thinking. Suddenly, I wanted to develop tough skin that could burn without my squirms, to cut a whole chicken. I wanted to be a girl who *wanted* to cook, a girl who *knew* how to cook. Suddenly, I saw the kitchen as a training ground; a space that allowed me to overcome fears like overcooking, undercooking, applying the wrong ingredients, adding incorrect measurements, and giving people food poisoning. I knew I had to take risks to learn how to cook, and I was thankful that my mother had the patience to teach a daughter who had been so eager to refuse. Her agitated shrieks and villainous chuckles were not torture, but tough love, her effort to encourage me to learn. They were an expression of my mother's love and concern, hoping the lessons would stick; hoping that one day, I would cook for myself, for my family, without fear.

Big Female Boy

We beat each other up like video game avatars, me and two boys who were family friends. They lived two blocks up from my house, and their mother loved having me over because I was the daughter she never had. She had four sons, after many failed attempts for a baby girl. Her husband died a few years after I had met him. Although we weren't related, I referred to her as Aunt Rose. In Malawi, it was common for girls to address elderly women as "auntie." It was a sign of respect. She often welcomed me with homemade cookies and cakes. She also never expected me to help out in the kitchen. I was free to hang around with her boys while she and her house boy, Wongani, cooked for us. Maybe she never asked me to do things because she didn't have experience with a daughter, or maybe it was because I wasn't her child. My mouth watered each time I set foot in her house. Delicious scents lured me straight to the kitchen. Sometimes, she cooked turkey for Thanksgiving. Her sons would tease her about celebrating American history that had nothing to do with Malawi. Aside from her love for turkey, I suspect she was trying to teach us about other cultures, about a land that most Malawians dreamed of visiting. Two of her sons, Lawrence and Chikondi, were close to my age.

I was eight, Lawrence was seven, and Chikondi was ten. When we played fighting games, Aunt Rose misunderstood when we beat each other to a pulp. Her instincts were always to defend me. She reprimanded her sons, asking them to treat me with respect, to see me as their own sister. But what Aunt Rose never knew was that I had become the kind of girl who was used to being beaten by boys— sometimes, I was the girl who sent boys home bleeding.

Our worlds were filled with war games, soccer and basketball tournaments, or we organized fighting contests to see which one of us was the strongest. We needed to know who could kick, punch, or do backflips and somersaults. We needed to know who could jump off a railing and fly like Superman or our favorite avatars from video games like *Street Fighter* or *Mortal Kombat*. Other times we sat on Smythe Road, a street outside their gate, singing popular hip-hop and R&B songs by Notorious B.I.G., Missy Elliot, Boyz II Men, and Tupac. Or we yelled nonsense at people who passed by, mostly goofy remarks to make them laugh. We were attention-seekers. But sometimes we attracted the wrong attention from three boys who bullied me—Mada, Zandiwe and Simon. Mada, a chubby light-skinned boy, had once called me an "ugly goat" and said that he found me disgusting. Zandiwe, a tall, dark-skinned boy with a hawk nose, had once set his dog to chase me down a dirt road with rocks that dug into my bare feet because I had won a race against him at school. Simon, a skinny, chocolate-brown skin boy with a clean-shaved head and dark mysterious eyes, always asked the girls I played with if I was *really* a girl because I dressed in baggy jeans and oversized t-shirts. According to Simon, I played like a boy, and he eventually coined a Chichewa phrase describing me as a "big female boy," *Chimtsikana cha chimamuna*—a phrase which was meant to suggest that I was an unattractive masculine girl.

The twist was that I was keen on playing with the same boys who bullied me. I had developed an obsession with finding ways to win challenges against boys because I felt just as strong as they were. At eight years old, I already believed that females could be as powerful as males, and I used every opportunity while playing to prove it. Growing up as a sporty tomboy was a double-edged sword. On the one hand, I was admired for my athletic spirit. Some kids were in awe of me, mesmerized by how I did daring things that most girls feared or failed to do—climbing big trees, leaping over dangerous pits, executing difficult basketball and soccer moves. On the other hand, some made fun of me for doing those same things, reflecting a child's tendency to be cruel, jealous or envious of others who might be different or better than them. I knew I had to do outrageous things to gain acceptance from boys, especially the ones who wished to dub me fickle when my strengths proved otherwise. I had to devise secret missions to show how tough I was, even if it meant bleeding.

Boys can be so indecisive. One day, I found Lawrence and Chikondi organizing a fighting contest. I greeted Aunt Rose inside the house and walked to her backyard verandah. There was a big circle of about fifteen to twenty little boys who looked my age. Some were standing, others sitting on the cement floor; a few sat on two metal railings that lined either side of a path that led to my aunt's green lawn. Her flower beds were flourishing with color, healthy big plants, and her maize garden was beaming green. Three of the boys were Mada, Zandiwe, and Simon. I almost backed away from the door at the sight of them. But defiance kicked in, my habit to remember that I was not supposed to look or behave scared if I wanted to play with boys. Not to mention, this was a chance to apply my secret mission. I stood at the door, holding the side of a maroon burglar bar, listening to Lawrence, the current ringleader, explain what was going to happen. Three fighting matches had already been set. The winners of each fight would battle one another in the final round. Only one person could win the contest.

"I want to fight too," I announced from the door.

All the boys turned to look at me. A cacophony of noise followed. My three bullies were the first to welcome me with insults.

Mada pointed at me, "Who invited stupid?"

Zandiwe flicked his hand, "Go home!"

Simon, with a devilish grin, "*Kaphike*! Doesn't mommy need someone to stir food in the pot?"

I frowned. Their words stung, but my legs wouldn't move. I held onto the burglar bar as if I was going to fall. *Stay. Don't move. You know how to stay*, I thought. Chikondi intervened.

"Shhh! My mom is in the house. She'll tell all of you to leave if we don't get along."

My bullies clucked, whispering things I could not hear. They knew they had to settle for peace if they wanted to be part of the contest.

"Carol can fight!" Chikondi shouted, trying to reassure everyone of my strength. "She's beaten Musa before." Musa was a skinny, mixed-race, quiet kid, a relative of Aunt

Rose's family, a boy I had once bloodied—something I always felt guilty about. I never liked fighting to gain acceptance, but as a child, I did anything I could for it. Chikondi told everyone about fights I had had with boys in the neighborhood—how I took kicks like a champ, standing tall after someone's leg slammed against my body; how boys pulled my braids and I still fought them off me; how I could slap a face silly, leaving defeated boys in tears. Lawrence chimed in, dropping names of those I had fought, those who walked away from challenges because I wouldn't cry or give up. This was how Lawrence and Chikondi stood up for their "sister."

The bullies did not cave in.

Mada: "I just don't fight girls!" he shouted, shaking his head.

Zandiwe: "She's tiny! We'll break her!" as his hand flapped like a wobbly piece of paper.

Simon: "I don't think this is a good game for a girl. Shouldn't you play with dolls?" with raised eyebrows.

I rolled my eyes. If Simon only knew how much I hated dolls. I didn't own any, and I made it clear to my parents that I hated them. I wanted toy guns and grenades instead, which they never bought for me. If one of my girlfriends asked me to play with dolls, I was curious about why Barbie was so perfect. Sometimes we cut Barbie's long hair. I liked that she wouldn't look like what people expected—a blue-eyed woman with long blonde hair, a perfect body, and a hot boyfriend. Upon our intervention, Barbies would be imperfect, like me, the tomboy in oversized clothes, the one who didn't fit in with other girls because of her boyish demeanor.

Simon had a different challenge for me. It was well-known that Simon's house had a little hill in his backyard. I had never seen it before, but rumor had it that the hill had green grass with rocks that protruded as if someone had designed a maze. Although it had caution written all over it, some boys saw it as a good challenge to ride to the bottom without falling off their bikes. Simon suggested a race downhill.

"Carol, you can do it if you have the guts," Simon said, smirking.

Silence. The boys fidgeted and looked at each other, but no one said anything.

I smiled at Simon. At last, a glimpse of hope that he saw me as someone worth challenging.

Simon continued, "If you break your legs, maybe that will keep you in the kitchen with your mom." He snickered, looking at other boys, searching for confirmation.

I looked away. My smile faded.

Another cacophony of noise—most of the boys discussed participating in the race. A few stared at me with doubtful smirks. I thought of what my mother would say if I came home with scars and bloody noses again. She was already at her breaking point with my endless wounds, begging me not to play rough games with boys. "Do you want to end up being a toothless girl?" she would ask while cleaning my wounds. Then, she warned me about having a collection of scars all over my body, that someday I would regret it. This was the concern of the same Lieutenant Mother who watched me burn my skin while cooking nsima. But those blisters usually blew up in a day or two and then faded. She wasn't worried about those wounds. I never responded to her warnings, but I rolled my eyes as I watched her gently dab off blood from my arms and legs. Almost every week, I had band-aids on my body, you would think I did it for strange and unconventional fashion purposes. At the rate I was going, if I didn't cover my arms with my school sweater, teachers would have asked if there was any type of child abuse at home. Those who noticed my bruises assumed it was from playing, which it was, but maybe not the kind of playing they expected a little girl to engage in. I didn't mind the blood. My secret missions to outdo boys in their own game were more important, and when Simon threw a bike challenge at me, when I listened to the silence of fearful boys, when I saw their doubtful smirks, it fired me up to be the first to accept the challenge.

"I'll do it!"

Immediately after my acceptance, three other boys agreed to take on the challenge. I didn't know any of them. My heart raced. I wasn't sure if I could make it down to the bottom of a rocky hill on my bike. It wasn't even a mountain bike—the kind that could switch gears, a bike with strong brakes that could decrease speed efficiently. Instead, I had a standard little girl's bike—pink and white, a set of metal brakes, big rubbery tires, and nothing more. It was the first bike my father ever bought for me. My other concern was that I didn't know how long it would take for my wounds to heal if I crashed into something. Body cuts and scrapes were something I was used to, but I didn't know how to handle a broken body part. I had never experienced that kind of hurt, and I blocked it out of my mind for the sake of my mission. My bullies had to witness how skilled I was. The thought of their faces watching me maneuver my way down a dangerous hill was enough for me to bypass the possibility of an accident. I accepted the challenge—with fear gripping my heart.

*

Simon unlatched the metal gate, dragging it to the side to let me and the fifteen-to-twenty boys into his yard. During our two-mile walk to Simon's house, the boys had been teasing me about my bike. They doubted it would make it down the hill.

They asked if I was afraid.

I lied that I wasn't.

They tried to persuade me to back out.

I said backing out was for cowards.

Mada said I would leave Simon's house with my face split in half.

I asked if that was why his face looked like it had once been split in half.

Zandiwe said it was a waste of time to compete with me.

I said it was obvious he was afraid to compete, and that was why *I* was doing the challenge and *he* wasn't.

"You're so stubborn!" someone shouted.

"I know," I whispered.

The gate was opened, and the boys rode their bikes towards Simon's backyard. It was my first time at his house, so I chose to walk my bike in instead of riding to an unknown destination. Simon's house resembled mine, a painted white brick house with a reddish-brown rooftop. There weren't many colorful flowers but tall, green banana-leaf plants, mango and guava trees, and the front yard had a neatly trimmed lawn, several cement pathways aligned with tiny brown pebbles leading towards the house. Simon closed the gate and ran up to me as I slowly pushed my bike in the direction where the boys had ridden. The hill was in the backyard.

"Carol! Are you ready to break your butt?" Simon snickered, hopping up and down.

He looked cute in his black Batman t-shirt and dark blue basketball shorts. I was in shorts and a t-shirt, too; with a flat chest and backside, I looked just like one of the boys. Only my braids, which were tied back, announced that I was female. Simon had gorgeous hazel-brown eyes and flawless light brown skin. I never saw scars on his body. His dark eyebrows, which were very close to his eyes, often made quick, defined shifts. Sometimes it was comical to watch him make different facial expressions. His eyes never opened wide, and when they moved from side to side, he looked like someone ready to do something naughty. I had a crush on Simon, and I never told anyone because I didn't know how to explain why I was falling for a boy who bullied me. I had decided that he was the nicest bully out of the three, and I could swear that sometimes I caught him eyeing me; not with a mean, condescending stare, but as if he was curious. Other times, he smiled at me as if he was hiding a sweet person behind his harsh treatment. Looking back, I wonder if his obsession with calling me a "big female boy" and inquiring if I was really a girl was because he didn't know how to feel about me. Is it possible that Simon had a crush on a girl who looked and behaved like a boy? And since in Malawi, boys were not meant to have crushes on other boys, Simon may have struggled with his feelings for a boyish-girl.

Seeing Simon at his home made me look at him differently, too, as if we were legitimate friends. It was his personal space, possibly a comfort zone, and how many people get to see their bullies at their own homes? I smiled at Simon out of courtesy, respecting the fact that he had allowed me to enter his yard, but I didn't respond to his question about my butt. I dismissed it as a scare tactic. All I could feel was the fright in my racing heart. If Simon heard it, he probably would have kicked me out of the race, insisting, while rejoicing, that I was too afraid to handle a challenge against boys. So I put on my poker face. I walked on.

The hill in the backyard was now in sight. Boys stood with their bikes at the top of the slope. The distance from the top to the bottom was longer and steeper than I had imagined. I panicked, stopping my bike to take in the distance of the slope—about a hundred meters, maybe more. *What on earth am I doing? Is it really that worth it?* A few boys mocked me in Chichewa from afar, something about "dying today." But some of them cheered and screamed my name. They sounded like sincere cheers. I assumed it was because I was about to do something daring. A little courage shot through my body. I had to complete the race. There were five of us in the challenge, and my competitors had modern mountain bikes that looked like they had seventeen gears ready to transform into planes if they needed to. The four competing boys were already at the starting line. I wheeled my bike to the side farthest from the spectators. Who knew if my three bullies would play a prank or shout obnoxious things to throw me off course. It was best to keep away and let them watch me from a distance.

Simon explained the rules. Everyone had to start at the same time. Disqualification if you begin the race before the word GO. No bumping bikes. No stopping in the middle of the slope. No talking during the race. The first one to cross the finish line wins. Our spectators cheered, jeered and applauded. I clenched the handles of my bike, my eyes swiftly searching for a safe path to take. No sign of one. Rocks jutted out in random places. This was no maze. It was nature in its own chaotic design, and safety was not part of its plan. Had anyone ever made it to the bottom? I hadn't even thought to ask the question, but now that I was looking at the lack of smooth ground, I had plenty of doubt that anyone had ever made it to the bottom.

I heard the word GO.

My right leg left the ground, allowing my bike to roll downhill, hands firmly planted on both handles and metal brake latches. I squeezed them slightly so my bike wouldn't lose control. Then, I began to dodge rocks. My bike moved along a path that curved from side to side. I was zig-zagging like a snake continuously reshaping itself. I heard muffled shouts and screams from Mada, Zandiwe, and Simon. Their voices were very distinct, but I could not make out their words. The only word I understood was "Iwe!" meaning "you." I figured they were probably insulting me. Something along the lines of "you stupid girl!" "you ugly goat!" Or Simon's favorite, "you big female boy!" For the most part, I went at the same speed as my four competitors. My heart pounded uncontrollably, palms sweaty. The bike felt like it was speeding up because my mind could no longer process the swiftness of its motion. I could no longer calculate safer paths. I stopped thinking. All I could do was dodge the protruding rocks as quickly as my reflexes could permit. Riding down in a vertical position, the air brushed against my skin. I became a machine. Dodging rocks this way and that. Then, I could no longer see any boys riding beside me. My focus was on my reflexes, trying my best not to stop in the middle of the hill. I let go of the bike, turning it from side to side, wherever and whenever I could. As I neared the bottom, my attention shifted to my mastery of fast turns, the swift rhythm of rolling downhill. I widened my focus. The bottom was less rocky. None of my opponents were near me. Maybe I was going very fast or maybe they had all fallen off or stopped their bikes in the middle of the slope. Spectators screamed my name, but this time they were encouraging me to keep moving, to "keep going!" Even my three bullies cheered me on.

My bike stabilized on flat ground. I grinned because I had made it to the bottom. I slowed down, giggling with pride. Secret mission complete. My bullies had witnessed it. I waved my right arm to show my pride in the victory. The boys were still cheering. The finish line was a few feet ahead, and the surface was flat enough for me to turn my head back for a second, just to watch the boys running down the hill, cheering me on, to see them see me cross the finish line.

And then, a sudden halt.

The front tire of my bike stuck to the ground like an arrow that landed after being shot, pivoting on a giant rock, sending my back tire into the sky. Next, I was flying over the handle bars like an untrained Superman. Then I rolled on the ground like a useless piece of junk someone had recklessly thrown across the lawn. The fall was such a shock that it felt like an out-of-body experience, as if I were watching myself slam against the ground, rocks scraping off my skin. The tumble didn't go on for too long, but when it ended, my adrenaline transformed any pain I may have felt to numbness. For a second, I laid flat on the ground, disoriented by the unexpected flying. I faced a blue sky with a congregation of white clouds. Then, I propped up my head and shoulders to see where I had landed. My bike was laying a few feet away from me like a twisted-up dummy. I looked at the ground and realized I was lying right on the finish line. I jumped up immediately, unshaken by the fall. The boys stared at me in shock, their hands covered their mouths, some scratched their heads not knowing what to do or say, some snickered, others tried to show a face of concern, struggling to stifle their urge to burst into laughter. Parts of my body ached, but my excitement for winning doused the pain. I smiled at my three bullies, then raised my arms as high as I could. I claimed my winning status. Everyone screamed my name.

No one had ever completed the race down the rocky hill. I learned this after I had won. I was finally receiving the respect I had always wanted. Some boys had claimed to win in the past but most of them had cheated by stopping mid-slope, comfortably re-routing to make it to the bottom. It was only a few minutes after the race was over that I started to feel pain on my right shoulder. When I lifted my t-shirt, there was a giant red bruise the size of Texas. My skin must have been ripped off when I rolled on the ground. My mother was *not* happy.

"You will regret this when you are older!" she shouted.

That night, my brothers made fun of me. They said I would grow up with an ugly shoulder. I sulked, ignoring them because they had no idea what I had accomplished that day. They had no idea that I had just succeeded at gaining acceptance from boys I wanted to play with every day. No idea that I had become a champion in the faces of bullies who underestimated me. I ate supper alone that night because I didn't want anybody to rob me of my feeling of triumph. Simon and I would become better friends after winning the race. There would be less vicious remarks from him. Mada and Zandiwe never stopped teasing me, but it was undeniable that they saw me as a force to be reckoned with whenever we played together.

My mother was right. The bruise never healed properly. I grew new skin, but it still looks like a scar, like a very bad burn. During my late teens and early twenties, I felt insecure when I wore tank tops or clothes that revealed my shoulders. As time progressed and age made me more comfortable with the imperfections of my skin, I began to accept the scar as part of me. It became my tattoo, a reminder of my fighting spirit. Whenever people stare at it, while pretending not to stare at it, the first words out of my mouth are, "eight years old. My victory tattoo." Courage was carved inside my DNA. I am sure there are other bloodless ways I could have chosen to prove that girls can be just as strong as boys, but that was just the kind of eight-year-old girl I was.

Child-Thief

The houses were known as servant's quarters. A row of small adjoined square rooms, giving the look of a long rectangular house, once white, now covered in a film of brown from years of dust. The walls were smeared with thick mud, charcoal-drawn graffiti everywhere. The tenants who rented them were lower-class families that had migrated from the villages, mostly young or middle-aged couples with one or two children. The rooms were not large enough for big families; four was the maximum capacity. We called them servant's quarters because most of the tenants worked as cooks, guards and gardeners for middle and upper-class families. Our house was next to the servant's quarters, separated only by our tall, brick fence and a dirt-road called West Drive, which merged with a tar-marked street leading to Aunt Rose's house on Smythe Road. Whenever my father's charcoal Peugeot 605 passed the quarters, children would chase after it, jumping up and down, waving their hands while screaming, "byeeee!" Some wore tattered clothes, dirty clothes, others semi-naked, barefooted, their faces covered in boogers or whatever they had been eating. I knew they lived a hard life, but I was always captivated by the joy and curiosity they showed, even for a passing car. They seemed happy. I wanted to know them.

I was a seven-year-old with a full-time job of sparking friendships with children from the quarters. When they stood near our gate, staring at me as though I were a creature from another planet, I showed them my toys. I threw my football at them or casually kicked it around, hoping they would run to pick it up and play with me. Sometimes, if I gathered enough courage, I would ask if they wanted to join me in a game. They often said yes, some nodding their heads enthusiastically while others sniffed mucus back into their noses, laughing among themselves as if I were insane to ask them. They called me *mwana wa bwana*, the boss' kid, or *mwana wa kumpanda,* the kid who lives in a yard. I also tried to win them over with candy, if my parents gave me pocket money. I became a Pied Piper they followed to purchase chewing gum, lollipops, and chocolates from the neighborhood vendors. They would circle around me and hold out their palms as I placed candy in each of their hands.

We played catch and kickball on the dirt road that separated our houses. I played barefoot, too, because I wanted them to see me as their equal. At times, we fought about cheating during games, or we disagreed about rules. We sulked, clucked, swore and taunted each other, "*choka iwe!*" "*galu iwe!*" "*shupiti!*" And when things got really nasty, we threw stones at each other from afar. Our arguments were usually resolved with no apologies. Instead, we resumed playing, without talking about our fights, after a few days of calming down. Their parents saw me as a kind girl because I brought sweets and toys for their children, and I was very quiet around them, often smiling coyly when they invited me over for lunch, four o'clock tea, when they offered me *mandasi* and *dzitumbuwa* to snack on. I always said no, fearing they would think I was a greedy, rich kid eating their food as if I didn't have enough at my own home. A part of me knew their kindness was sincere, but I couldn't shake off my paranoia. I did, however, enjoy listening to their stories about village life. My mind exploded with flashes of their tales; how they experienced voodoo curses, mysterious illnesses, nightly visits from *afiti*, their attempts to break witchcraft spells, and their descriptions of *Gule Wamkulu*, secret cults that performed dance rituals in public. I prayed that nobody would curse my family. The tenants at the quarters may have lived in buildings covered in dirt, they may have been struggling to make ends meet, but they knew hospitality. They had an abundance of heart and humbleness, and the more I hung around them, the more I felt like I had an extended family. This is the reason I will never understand why I had to steal from them.

*

Next to the servant's quarters was a small garden where they grew vegetables and corn. It wasn't a big field, and it wouldn't take anyone long to count all the cornstalks. One year, the tenants in the quarters planted their corn earlier than most people. It wasn't a race to grow crops, but every time my step-niece, Mphatso, and I passed their garden, we envied how green their cornstalk leaves looked. It was ready to be plucked. Mphatso was two years older than me, taller, dark-skinned with small, dark-brown eyes. My parents grew their own corn, but theirs was not ready for harvest. They owned three big fields where they grew different fruits, beans, mkhwani, peas, bonongwe, often selling their harvest. They made the most money from selling corn. Every year, they harvested about 150 bags of corn, 50KG each.

It was around 5 PM when the sun had begun to set and the streets were growing dark. Mphatso and I were running home from our friend's house, turning the corner from Smythe Road to West Drive. We had been running for over fifteen minutes, and I could feel sweat building in my jeans. We stopped frequently, panting, trying to catch our breath. As we got closer to the quarters near my house, two little boys in shorts and unbuttoned collared shirts started heckling us in Chichewa.

"It's getting dark, little girls! Hurry home or you'll get beaten!" one of them shouted.

"*Choka iwe!*" I yelled, asking them to go away.

The boys proceeded to chase after us along the dirt road that separated the quarters from our house. The dark of night was taking over and we couldn't see the faces of the boys, but we could hear them laughing. I hated being laughed at, and something in my mind concluded that they were boys we had fought before during our play. Maybe scaring us was their revenge.

"Let's go and steal their corn," I said, panting.

"Why?" Mphatso asked, struggling to catch her breath, too.

"Because I'm craving it, and those boys are stupid," I coughed, still trying to control my breathing.

We walked slowly near the quarters. A few people had made fires to cook dinner, but all we could see were flames glowing from afar. Everything was quiet in the field. I slipped into a row of cornstalks, reaching out my hand for an ear of corn. I plucked one. Mphatso shuffled around next to me.

"Did you get one?" she whispered.

"Yes. You?" I held my breath.

"I have two."

"How many should we take?"

"I don't know."

"Not too many," I said, "We need to leave some for them."

The boys had followed us, maybe because they never saw the gate to my house open and close. They must have known we were still out on the dirt road. They whispered in the dark. I held my breath, knelt down and froze with two corncobs in my hands.

"Ah-Ahhh!" one of them shouted. "*Akuba*! They're stealing our corn! We'll tell on you!"

My heart began to race. At first, I thought to stay silent, hoping they would think they were mistaken and go away. But the silence frightened me more.

"No, we aren't!" I shouted back. "We are hiding from you idiots! Why are you chasing us?"

No response.

"Why do you want to hit us?!" I asked.

No response.

"We have to get out of here!" Mphatso whispered, ruffling through the cornstalks.

"I'm throwing mine away," I said, dropping the corn. Next, we bolted at full speed towards my house. I picked a rock and banged on a metal rod at the corner of the gate.

"It's us!" I shouted for the guards. "Let us in, fast-fast! There are boys chasing us!"

The guard opened the gate. "What are you running from?" he asked. The concern in his voice was that of a person ready to protect us from whatever was after us. His dark blue overalls blended in with his dark skin, and with night all around us, all we could see were his eyes and teeth. We told him that big scary boys threatened to beat us, but we ran on to avoid more questions. Mphatso opened the kitchen door. I flew in first, running straight to my bedroom. Then, we shut the door, and threw ourselves on my bed, panting.

"Do you think they told on us?" I asked.

"I don't know," Mphatso snickered, coughing a little.

"Maybe they left when we were silent."

"Yeah, maybe."

"I doubt they would tell on us," I said, lifting my body from the waist up, "*They* were chasing *us*!"

"*Yeah*," Mphatso agreed as if we were defending ourselves in front of a judge, "*They* started it!"

The next few minutes were filled with defenses, justifications that made us feel better about our robbery. We declared the two boys guilty. *They* were wrong to threaten us. *They* were wrong to chase us. *They* would be convicted because of a lack of proper explanation for provoking girls. *They* would be convicted "bad boys" who beat girls. We laughed, cackling while high-fiving at how comedic it all was. Then, we boasted about the big corncobs we had discovered in the field, how we had told off the boys, how fast we had run from them—both of us, unstoppable.

There was a knock at my bedroom door. We hushed our snickering. Dave, our cook, was sent to summon us.

"*Akuti mupite*," he said, telling us to go to the kitchen.

Mphatso and I glanced at each other. I shook my head, debating whether to answer or pretend we weren't in the room.

"Let's go," Mphatso said. "Relax, maybe mom just wants us to cook."

True. Sometimes my mother asked Dave to make sure we were home by 5 PM and in the kitchen, cooking. We walked slowly past the living room. I looked in the corner, at a half-naked sculpture of a Ngoni hunter with bulging eyes and a wide-open mouth. He looked like he knew what we had done and was very upset. I clucked at him, annoyed. No one was around, and the T.V. was off. I opened the kitchen door. My mother's stern face told me everything I needed to know. Trouble. When our eyes met, she shook her head, giving us a condescending stare, a look which only surfaced if she had heard either shocking or absurd news. Then, I heard voices coming from outside. My father was talking to a man, but I didn't know who it was.

"Both of you sit down," my mother said, pointing at chairs around the rectangular table at the center of the kitchen. Mphatso and I sat quietly, heads down. I avoided eye contact with my mother whom I could feel glaring at us, eavesdropping at the conversation that was happening outside.

"*Pepani*," I heard my father apologizing. "Have a good night. We will resolve this, *bwana*." My father called men "bwana" because he believed that everyman was the "boss" of his household. He walked slowly towards the kitchen door and stood looking at us. He was wearing navy blue shorts and a cream t-shirt. Thick veins bulged from his hairless athletic legs. I took one look at his face, which now resembled the look my grandfather used to make with exorcizing eyes, and like a reflex, I bounced up from my chair with fright. Mphatso stood up, too. His cheeks had dropped, eyes red, a stare with no blinks. His wagging finger looked longer than it actually was—like one of the wooden school rulers that teachers used to hit the palm of our hands when we were being punished. My father was angry.

"But I told Carol…!" Mphatso began as if my father had asked her a question.

My father's lips tightened like someone about to spit out vicious words.

"*Zoona, mwana iwe!* How dare you steal corn from other people's fields!" He shouted, then charged after us. Mphatso and I circled the table. My father followed, tossing aside each chair that was tucked under. We circled and circled, sometimes we held on to the table then shifted from side to side to trick my father into running in the wrong direction. This was a rare sight. I did *not* like this version of "Catch Me If You Can."

"Do I not grow enough corn for this family?" His voice boomed as he stood still for a while. Sweat built around his forehead. "I said *why* must you rob other people! Are you dying of hunger?" he charged again.

The table made loud screeching noises each time it shifted. At one point, Mphatso knew to break the cycle of running around it. She ran outside of the house. I, on the other hand, had too much fear to think of it sooner. My father started moving the table to one corner, eliminating the space that allowed us to run around. A giant space formed at the center of the kitchen. This would lead him directly to me.

"I'm sorry, Dad! Boys were trying to beat us!" I screamed, panting, trying to sob, but the shock of the chase had frozen my tears.

My father heard none of it. "Do you want to start a rumor that Mr. Kautsire is raising little thieves? Come *here*!" he shouted, pointing at the floor.

My father had never laid a hand on me, but that day I did not trust him. I bolted outside.

*

We ran in the dark, pushing through thick, stuffy layers of the night's air. Although running around the house gave me a better chance of escaping my father, I had another problem. Dogs. I was scared of them. We had just bought two, brown medium-sized mutts, and sometimes they growled at me when I walked near them. These were untrained dogs that slept outside the house to help the guards with night watch. In other words, they could tear you apart if they wanted. My parents had them chained during the day until they started getting used to us. The guards never seemed to fear dogs, and they grew fond of each other quickly. I never knew what their secret was. The dogs chased after me, barking. It was my second lap around. I screamed, now sobbing as I tried to run faster. I turned my head to the side, looking back to see how far the dogs were. I failed to catch a glimpse of them because I also feared to fall. Lying on the ground as "dog dinner" was the last result I wanted. All I heard was barking.

I had lost track of my father. The barking ceased before my third lap. One of the guards had called the dogs away. I reduced speed when I reached the kitchen door. My father was nowhere to be seen. I stood at the entrance and peeked inside the kitchen. Mphatso was washing the silver pot we used to cook nsima. She pointed vigorously at the living room door, signaling where my father had gone. My mother was seated behind the table, which was back in its proper center position. At the sight of me, she shook her head and leaned on the table, arms crossed.

"*Zoona*, Carol? Do you go to steal corn from the quarters? You have made us look like bad people. Your father is very upset!"

I couldn't look at my mother. My body trembled from adrenaline. I stared at the floor instead, wiping the sweat from my forehead.

"You say you can't sleep at night because of *akuba*, but now look who the thief is?"

I gave no response.

"Don't you play with the children from the quarters? Don't you chat with their parents?"

No response.

"You have really embarrassed us, Carol. Don't ever do that again!"

I lifted my head slowly, tightening my lips because of frustration. I nodded. My head was pounding.

"You have to apologize to your father and the people in the quarters."

I nodded.

"Now help Mphatso cook nsima," she said, rising from her chair. She walked toward the living room.

Mphatso and I cooked in silence. A few times, we tried to address what had happened, mostly our amazement with how my father chased us, a rare thing to see in the Kautsire household. It was easier to talk about my father than to face what we had done wrong. Yet, shame had already begun setting in. Each time we laughed about the incident, sadness also weighed heavily. My mind condemned me with guilt for robbing people who were kind to me. I had also become my own worst nightmare, a thief who robs people at night. A hypocrite. After cooking, I went to my room and never came out for the rest of the night. I refused to eat supper, feeling unworthy of the privilege to eat food. When I lay in bed, my mind was tormented by images of me hiding in cornstalks, two corncobs in my hands, robbing people who had struggled for it, people who had shown me hospitality, people who had treated me like family. That night, I convicted myself. *I* was the guilty one. *I* was wakuba. *I* was the "bad girl" who stole.

Playing With the Eucharist

Understanding religion came through a lot of silly childish adventures with Mphatso. I wanted to know more about God, but being exposed to different religions made God so confusing for me. I knew that Malawi had a lot of Catholics and Muslims, and there were other religions that I never took the time to understand. Yet since the age of seven, my desire to be part of the many who believed in God made me take risks that were either disrespectful or I simply didn't know what I was doing.

Once, my parents sent Mphatso and me to deliver some food and provisions at the nuns' convent. We lived a few miles away from the convent that was at the top of a dirt road near our church. Mphatso and I climbed the hill, chattering as usual when we arrived at a maroon gate. We banged the metal with a rock, so the guard could open it. Once inside, a few nuns came to greet us and led us to the living room. There was a wooden rectangular coffee table at the center and the sofas and chairs had flowery doilies on them.

The nuns gave Mphatso and me Fanta soda with unblessed Eucharist. These were leftovers from the blessed round Eucharist that people take in church. Mphatso and I didn't know what to make of it. My mind raced at the thought of eating Christ's body with a soda. When the nuns left the room, Mphatso and I recited what the priest said during mass in Chichewa, "Mudzina la Yesu Khristu," then we lifted the Eucharist in the air to honor it and placed it in our mouths. We snickered at our self-held mass—something which we partly knew was disrespectful. Yet being children, our conflict to be respectful and skeptical was very skewed.

Even during confession, Mphatso and I would plan what to say ahead of time. We would take an inventory of our sins and rehearse how to confess them with earnest faces. We wanted to look like children who were truly sorry, so we practiced drooping our faces, blinking slowly as if we were at the verge of tears. It was a chance to ask God to forgive me for stealing corn from the servant's quarters, for beating up little boys just to fit in, for disobeying my mother when she tried to teach me how to cook. I even cut deals with God that if he forgave me, I would stop being a professional beer-sipping con artist who gulped down any beer glass I found abandoned by an adult. The thought of being forgiven excited us. We would leave our sins with the priest to intercede for us with God. Our spirits would be clean and blessed again. The day I finished my catechism classes, I was dressed in all white—a long-sleeved blouse, a pleated skirt, and Maryjane shoes. I looked like an angel ready to make my way to heaven. I stood in a line with other kids who were prepared to receive Christ's Eucharist. It was a hot day and the wait took forever but I made it to the priest looking as pious and as innocent as I could. When it came time to confess, I was on my knees as the priest leaned closer to me to hear my sins. My mind drew a blank. Everything I had planned with Mphatso was forgotten. Instead, I said things like, "Forgive me, father, because I stole ndiwo from the pot." Something that wasn't true at all. But fear had taken over and the result was spewing nonsense just to get through confession, without a clue who God really was. Since I was a child, I hoped the priest would buy my lies, and as I knelt down in front of parents and friends, I held my hands together while the priest nodded to my fake sins—sins I was ashamed of making up, sins I don't even remember until today.

*

I flashback to times when Mphatso and I attended village catholic masses before we had finished our catechism classes, just waiting for the part when Eucharist was taken. I remember sitting in a crowd of villagers near dark-brown muddy houses, as the priest blessed the village with afternoon prayers. Our naughty friend, Mavuto, from next door, would accompany us. She was a tall and skinny dark-skinned girl who was known for dishing out profanity and fighting with people who came in her way. I may have had a reputation of being stubborn but Mavuto was notorious for being mean. Mphatso and I sat patiently, waiting for Mavuto's reveal of blessed Eucharist. So when it was time to take the Eucharist, she joined the line to receive it and saved it in her mouth to show us what it looked like. When I saw the mushy Eucharist, I wondered if God would smite Mavuto with thunder for her unholy act. It looked like a soggy piece of bread. I wondered if Mavuto was feeling holy as she continued to chew it with pride. Her eyes were closed as if she was tasting the most delicious piece of bread. I knew she was doing it to show off and, indeed, I envied her at that moment because she had done something that allowed her to be closer to God. But who knew if this was true about a girl who hadn't even finished her catechism classes. I had to find out for myself.

I joined the line to receive the Eucharist. Fear flooded my mind with what God was thinking about the unholy gesture I was about to pull off. I looked at the crowd I was standing in, mostly villagers, women in their chitenjes, head-wraps, men and boys in shorts and trousers. Because my father, as a chairman of the St. Montfort parish, attended many Catholic gatherings, I worried that he would show up and catch me. I stepped closer and closer in line. Three people in front. Two. One. Then me. The priest raised the Eucharist.

"Mudzina la Yesu Khristu," he said.

"Amen," I replied as I held out my hands for him to place the Eucharist in my palms. Then, I ran back to meet Mphatso and Mavuto. We shared our triumphs in acquiring Eucharist. I bit into mine with fear, wondering if I was placing a part of Jesus inside of me or if God was upset with me for eating Christ's body without finishing catechism classes. It was like eating a tasteless waffle, and nothing in me changed after eating it. All I developed from my unholy act was fear that I had done something wrong.

By the time I had finished my catechism classes, the priest was supposedly giving me my first blessed Eucharist, but I had already experienced what I had in the village ceremony. I didn't know if this was a good or bad thing, but it is something that has bothered me for many years, something I felt I needed to write out as a truer confession than what I told the priest in front of a crowd of friends and family.

Just Like My Mother

My mother had figured out a way to make not only a grown man cry but the first President of Malawi, the late Doctor Hastings Kamuzu Banda. She was performing in a play called *Dziko La Nyanja*, Land of the Lake. The name and message of the show were in reference to a Malawi that was once called "Nyasaland," the old British Protectorate. Malawians took pride in their "Lake Malawi," which was also known as "Lake Nyasa," the ninth largest lake in the world, bordering the East African rift between Malawi, Mozambique, and Tanzania. In the middle of one of her scenes, the President was seen shedding tears, which my mother never saw while on stage but she learned later. Something in my mother's performance had triggered catharsis. President Banda was a man who had spoken against British colonialism and advocated for Malawi's independence, which was achieved in 1964. After enduring Western-European assumptions that Malawi, being a third world country, had uncivilized people with no talent, the President was thrilled to witness otherwise in *Dziko La Nyanja*. He was proud of his people.

My mother often told me this story when we watched movies with strong black females, such as Whoopi

Goldberg, Pam Grier, and Viola Davis. Just like me, with the "Oh, *hell* no!" expression and my fascination with how free American women seemed, she would marvel at any traces of strength and intelligence in their performances, their ability to adopt character traits that may or may not have had anything to do with who the actresses were in real life. She would gasp from her seat, one hand pressed against her chest, the other pointing at the T.V., "Carol, look-look-look!" Then, she commented on their dramatic facial expressions, the shape of their bodies, the way clothes fit them well. Taken back by their big uninhibited gestures, how they swirled their heads with attitude when they spoke. If they became outrageously loud with other characters, if they cursed, cried or clowned, she spoke of the impact it had on her.

"It's as if they're not acting," she would say, believing in characters as though they were people in real life. When their performances moved her, she remembered how *she* moved others. "I made the President *cry*?" she would say, questioning her own ability in disbelief, "I couldn't believe it when people told me." Then, she would smile, her head shaking from side to side, eyes transfixed, hypnotized by the performance of an actress on T.V.

I couldn't believe it either. The more I heard this story, the more I observed how she admired black women on T.V., the more I wanted to become an actress. There was power in performing, and it made people feel different kinds of emotions, just like my mother had done with the President. I wanted that power, too. I wanted to learn how to move people.

A budding actress in her late teens, my mother was 5'6, with a slim yet shapely body, glowing honey-brown skin, and an afro. Think Foxy Cleopatra. During her high school years, most people noticed her sharp, vibrant personality, the way she sang and swing danced in public, as if no one was watching. She loved The Beatles, The Beach Boys, Harry Belafonte and swooned over Elvis Presley. She was also one of the smartest girls in her high school cohort. It was no surprise that she was asked to perform in school plays, and she did it for most of her junior and senior year. When acting coaches from the United Kingdom visited her school, they became enamored with her charming voice, how well she spoke English, how beautifully she sang. They marveled at her fluid, graceful, body movement. She made dancing look simple and exciting. She was a free-spirit on and offstage, unlike most girls who feared to make a fool of themselves for the sake of art. A white middle-aged man named Mr. Cook was eager to recruit my mother. The plan was to fly her to the United Kingdom to study and develop her acting craft. It would be a dream come true for my mother, a step closer to becoming the film star she had always wanted to be. This was also a time when my grandfather was doing everything he could to put my mother through school—something that was shunned by the people in their town.

Getting an education had a bad reputation. My mother was mocked. There were rumors that if she pursued her studies, she would end up becoming a prostitute. This was backward thinking, similar to how European women in the

17th century were not allowed to read books. Society feared that book knowledge would seduce them to engage in scandalous sexual affairs. Other rumors involved fear of white people. In my mother's case, rumor had it that Mr. Cook was only recruiting her to be his slave. If he got enough of her, he might even proceed to kill her and eat her. Yes, to *eat* her. When some Malawians did not understand the differences between the looks and lifestyles of blacks and whites, they resorted to accusations of cannibalism. I suppose these were residual effects of British colonialism. Whites, with their history of dominating blacks, were thought of as man-eating monsters. The same applied to Asians; only *they*, according to some, ate dogs, too.

Gossip about my mother grew vicious. Her town swarmed with multiple versions of horrible things that would happen to her if she seized her opportunity in the U.K. The main pushers of the rumors were old-fashioned, conservative, black men and women, who did not believe in separating a child from Malawian traditions and culture. To them, education led children astray. Books were only digressions from learning about their culture, not to mention the sinful temptations of British and American music and television—the sinful swing dancing that seduced boys to touch girls inappropriately with hand-pulls, body-twists, and body-tosses over their shoulders. This included the vulgar rock n' roll music that encouraged sex, enticing children to gyrate both in public and behind closed doors. My mother, who was already labeled guilty of all the above, would not only be disgraced by Mr. Cook through physical abuse, prostitution, and cannibalism, but she would also shame my grandparents. They would be made examples of evil Malawians with no morals. My grandmother couldn't handle the rumors. She often rebuked my grandfather about damaging my mother with education. My grandfather ignored everything. He believed in education, after all, he was a school teacher himself. He never gave up on my mother, and *she* never gave up on education either.

When Mr. Cook asked what my mother's final decision was for the acting opportunity in the U.K., my mother lied. She gave a fake excuse that her parents did not want her to leave Malawi because they would miss her—an excuse sparked by fear of other people's ignorance, that dimmed the light of her dream to become a star. For many years, my mother became a more subdued woman because of this. Cooking, cleaning, and Malawian traditions for weddings, baby showers, bridal showers, and church events became her world. For a while, she would hide her potential to become more until fate unfolded a different path for her, a path that would unleash her free-spirit again. As an airhostess, she would become a traveling woman. Years later, she would marry my father, build a big house in Sunny Side and own a successful flower business. My mother is the funniest person in my family, the one who makes us laugh uncontrollably. She still goes nuts about The Beatles and The Beach Boys, and when Elvis's music plays, she leaps up, holding her hands high, clicking her fingers to the tune while swaying her body from side to side. For years, she mourned the loss of her dream and could only reminisce about how close she came to fulfilling it, but she also became a mother who was supportive of me—a daughter with a similar path to become an actress.

"It was God's plan for me to do for you what others failed to do for me," she would say while giving me a side hug on my bed, squeezing my body, holding me closer to her. I would nod, smiling. But I ached for her at the same time, thinking how brave she was to encourage another person towards the dream she had lost. Yet to my mother, it was as if life had given her a second chance, an encore to be strong for me and to stand by me when others doubted my passion for acting. She believed in me and my desire to become an actress living in America one day. And I was lucky to have a mother who would help me fight for my dream, to entertain people, to make them feel things, to move them, just as she had done with President Kamuzu Banda.

*

"Acting is not a real career," my father would say. Unlike my mother and me, what he watched on T.V. was purely for entertainment purposes or world news, and he rarely remarked on how an actor's performance impacted him. Well, there were two exceptions: Sidney Poitier and Morgan Freeman. If you mentioned the movies, *To Sir, With Love*, *Guess Who's Coming to Dinner* or *Lean On Me,* my father would be over the moon about discussing how remarkable it was for black men to tackle race and education conflicts with strong character. Their demeanor in movies was very similar to my father's—tall, slender men with well-cut hair, intelligent, with a stoic look and fingers that are ready to wag at naughty students. To me, at nine years old, my father was the same—a man with words full of wisdom and rhetorical questions about education. It made sense that my father was drawn to actors like Poitier because he saw a part of himself in them. Not to mention Morgan Freeman's strong resemblance to my grandfather. An exact copy.

"Whose face do you see?" My father would ask my mother, pointing at Morgan Freeman performing on T.V.

"You would think we are looking at your father," she said, smiling.

"Just like my father," he said, with a glow in his eyes.

If you remove Poitier and Freeman from the scene, acting was just like play to my father. It wasn't a real job. We argued about it a lot. This was our routine: my father would sit on the sofa in the living room, swirling his glass of Premier Brandy, and I would run around the furniture like an FBI cop, hiding behind sofas, wooden Ngoni sculptures, pretending to shoot imaginary villains. I would shout things I had heard on television, "Cover me, I'm going in!" or, "Bruce, I need back up now!" or dive into random spaces and dodge bullets like Keanu Reeves in *The Matrix*. These antics were always followed by my bold declaration that I would become a famous actress. Then, my father would chuckle and take a swig of his brandy.

"No, Ms. Kautsire. Become a doctor or a lawyer. That's where the money is. No one can touch you with those jobs, my dear," he would say, walking away from any fiery protests against him. I was relentless about avoiding careers I was not interested in.

"I don't want to end up feeling dead inside!" I would scream at his back (it was a phrase I had also heard characters yell on T.V.). Then, I ran off to find my mother.

My father's rejection cut deep. It hurt me to know that the man I wanted to impress the most was not proud of my passion for something that made me feel alive. It made sense that he would want me to be a doctor or a lawyer because a lot of Malawians valued those careers. They were respectable jobs, maybe because of the complexity of required tasks. Teaching, too. But not acting. I knew this didn't mean I couldn't become an actress, yet I wondered why my father was not more concerned about my happiness. I knew that living in a third world country like Malawi made people more desperate to find ways to make money, but weren't parents supposed to care about their children's happiness too? Each time he shunned my desire to act, I questioned how much he cared about me. Sometimes, my mother came to the rescue if she caught him in his disapproval. "*Inu*, leave my child alone!" she would say. "My baby is going to be a film star one day." I would run and collapse in her arms. She held me tightly, stroking my hair. Sometimes I cried, or I simply gave into the warmth of her embrace, the way she gently rocked me from side to side, strengthening me with her whispers.

"Don't worry, Carol. Don't listen to him. You are my star."

Kamuzu Academy

I started high school at the age of nine at a co-educational boarding school called Kamuzu Academy. Most people called it K.A. It was founded in 1981 by Doctor Hastings Kamuzu Banda, our first president and the man for whom my mother had once performed. The school was built in Mtunthama, 150 kilometers north of Lilongwe, the city where I was born. Its classic academic design featured a series of brown brick buildings, elegant curved archways, carefully tended green lawns, cement pathways and a gorgeous ornamental lake (teeming with monitor lizards!). This famous postcard image attracted many visitors. I reckon when President Banda built the Academy, he had Harvard University in mind.

When K.A. first opened, children from all over Malawi took the entrance exam, and only three students from every district were accepted. Things eventually changed. Entrance exams were still held, but they started accepting a larger number of students than three. When my parents signed me up to take the exams, many people said nine was too young to start high school. Other parents thought it was torture to impose advanced education on a young mind. Yet, my standard five teacher, Mr. Chiniko, thought I was smart enough to skip a few classes. During Parent's Day at South End Primary School, Mr. Chiniko, a short, fat man with gray hair and reading glasses he liked to sag on his nose, approached my parents and told them to sign me up for the K.A. entrance exams.

"She is bright. She deserves to go to the best school in Malawi," he said.

My parents took his advice.

Even today, I don't recall what was on the exams, but I remember panicking and looking to my right, at a colored girl named Brenda who seemed to be sailing through the exam effortlessly. That was the moment I started to feel self-conscious about my intelligence. Would high school be the beginning of my struggles with school? Would I suddenly be rendered average unlike the smart student I was used to being in primary school? Were my parents, indeed, making a mistake? I didn't know. But I passed the exams. When my father came home and told me the good news, I rushed to my parents' bedroom to tell my mother.

"Ma! Ma!" I shouted from the corridor. "Mommy, I passed! I'm going to K.A!" I burst through her bedroom door and leapt onto the bed. "I won't live here anymore! I'm a big girl now!" I shouted, hopping up and down, tossing pillows in the air.

"Congratulations! Eh-eh, that's nice!" she smiled, sitting at the edge of the bed. "But get down from there, you know your father."

My confidence in my intelligence was revived. This was a sign that Mr. Chiniko was right. My parents weren't crazy for sending me to a boarding school at nine. It was clear that I was not an average kid after all.

*

The trip to Kamuzu Academy was a test of my patience. I could not wait to start my new life, to be the adult I had always wanted to be. My bags were packed with all my favorite clothes. Mostly jeans and t-shirts with my favorite designer brands—Nike, FUBU, and adidas everything. My brother, Trevor, had taught me well about fashion, even though it was geared towards boys. Another suitcase was packed with food I had seen Charles take when going to K.A. (that was one relief for my parents, I would have a brother who was already enrolled at K.A.). For food, I took cookies, chips, ramen noodles, sardines, baked beans, canned cornbeef, *Kamba Puffs,* cornflakes, and candy. The school had a meal plan for us, but food from home was for our own snack time. I was ready to take care of myself. We left Blantyre early in the morning and throughout the journey, I couldn't stop imagining what Kamuzu Academy would be like. I thought about the things I wasn't exposed to, like the school discos Charles had told me about. I imagined cute boys coming to ask me for a dance. Would I be a "hot chick" or the girl who boys try to avoid? I thought of how sharing a room with a friend would be like a sleepover every night. What kind of mischief would we be up to at the Academy? I wondered what clothes girls would wear, if there would be any tomboys like me. *Are Mom and Dad really okay with me living with so many boys?*

We stopped in Lilongwe to have lunch after a four-hour drive. My impatience started to kick in and the sulking began.

"I'm not hungry!" I announced from the backseat. "Let's just keep driving."

"Carol, we need to eat," my mother said, looking behind from the passenger seat. "Your father has been driving for hours. He needs to rest."

She made sense. And I hated that she made sense. Why did she have to be so thoughtful at such an inconvenient time for me? I had a date with destiny, and my adrenaline for boarding school had taken over my mind. I wasn't tired, I wasn't hungry, and time seemed to stop since we arrived at the restaurant. As I watched my parents eat their food, I reprimanded them about slow-eating.

"Why don't you just take the burgers and eat them on the way?"

"Carol, you will get to Kamuzu Academy. We won't be long," my mother reassured me. I could see the slight wince in her smile. A part of me wondered if she was secretly sad that her nine-year-old child was leaving home. There was something about her eyes, the long stares she gave me as if to study my face for hidden feelings that revealed a deeper truth than my eagerness to leave her and my father. I continued to watch them eat, but frustration was written all over my face. Sometimes I muttered impatient remarks while staring at my surroundings, "This will make us so late," "I'll be the last kid to arrive," "I'll get suspended for arriving late." My parents could hear me. They ate in silence with peculiar smiles sealed on their faces, each one staring deeply into their food as if the burgers were fortune globes. I wasn't sure what they were thinking, but after some time, my mother lifted her head and looked at both my father and me. Suddenly Lieutenant Mother emerged, firing her signature questions:

"*Koma inu*, what kind of child gets so excited about going to boarding school?"

My father laughed. I gave no response. Too busy sulking.

My mother fired again:

"What kind of child gets so excited about leaving her parents?"

I slowly turned my head to look at her face. *There* was the look of puzzlement, as if she was looking at something inside of me that was incomprehensible. The look I had seen many people give me if I did something unusual. Was it strange for a nine-year-old to want to leave home in order to live with strangers? Did my mother understand that it wasn't about her but my desire to live like an adult? Something was weighing my mother down, and this time, the questions about what kind of girl I was, were not for me to answer, but for her to accept. My heart suddenly felt heavy. This was the moment when I knew there was pain behind our smiles, laughter, and awkward silences. This was the moment I felt the trip become bittersweet. This was the moment when I knew I would miss my parents, too.

*

At Kamuzu Academy, we wore preppy style uniforms—gray skirts (trousers for boys), cream-colored long-sleeve shirts, green ties with slanted gold lines, green sweaters with gold V-neck linings, cream-colored long socks, and black shoes. I liked the idea of being in school

101

uniform because we all looked the same. There was no competition for who looked the most attractive. But girls being girls, the battle of looks was in what you did with your hair and how short your skirt was. The ideal for K.A. was to have your skirt below the knees, but many of us had them tailored just above the knees. This usually got us in trouble with teachers, but we preferred the risk of showing a little knee because that was a trigger for boys to admire girls. Having a reputation of being "hot" was important in high school. And since the tender age of nine, I learned how to amplify my hotness through clothes and hairstyles. Of course, I often failed because my tomboy qualities would come raging out on some days. And other days, I borrowed clothes from friends—anything sexier than my jeans and oversized t-shirts.

One can say British colonial influence was deeply interwoven in Malawian culture, and it offered me structure and orderliness. I had a fixed routine at the Academy; classes ran from morning to 3 PM, sports for the rest of the afternoon and homework after dinner. Since I spent more months of the year at K.A., I became more accustomed to life at school than wearing chitenjes and cooking at home. I came to love theater and dance and dreamed of performing Shakespeare's plays. I particularly enjoyed singing British church hymns in assembly—"I Vow to Thee My Country," "O for a Thousand Tongues to Sing," "Here I am Lord,"— my favorite three hymns. Mr. Goodson, a tall, skinny, British white man, held choir rehearsals. This was the man who taught us about music notes and how to harmonize our singing. I was never a great singer, but in a room full of curious teenagers, the morale for music rubbed off on me.

It wasn't long before I found myself belting high notes while Mr. Goodson flamboyantly waved around his long arms and legs as choir master. He also taught us the classics, both Latin and Greek. I loved his teaching style because he was uninhibited when he moved around the classroom and he was always passionate and assertive about what he taught us. Although we often made fun of him for his quirky demeanor, we knew he was a good man to learn from. He had the drive and patience of someone concerned about the quality of our learning experience. Yet, we never failed to play pranks on him. Once, we locked him outside the classroom and planned to stare at the board, ignoring his desperate attempts to catch our attention as he waved his hands wildly outside the window.

"Open the door right now!" he hollered with his British accent. "I said open it now or you're all on detention!" he threatened.

None of us looked at the window. We just snickered and pretended he wasn't there. When we finally opened the door, he had had enough. First, he interrogated us, finding us guilty for locking the door based on our facial expressions: "Kevin, with your naughty look! I bet you did it!" he said, eye-balling a Kevin who could not contain himself with laughter. "Tamanda, with your rosy cheeks! Did you do it?" he shrieked, glaring at her face. "What about Kumbukani with your sinister smile?" he pointed as if he had caught him in the act. This went on for a few more minutes and none of us revealed who did it. I don't even remember who actually locked the door, but as long as you were sitting inside the classroom, you were in on the prank. Mr. Goodson was used to being teased, but this prank drove him to put the whole class on detention. For days, we pampered Mr. Goodson with kind and impressive remarks, anything that would let him know that we cared for him:

"Goodey, you're an excellent teacher!"

"Goodey, [insert Latin words to show you learned something from his class]."

"Goodey, *shapu*! What's up?" as if we were close friends in good terms again.

Within a few days, Goodey caved. His beloved students had redeemed themselves. I will admit that although I laughed with my friends about being punished for mischief, a part of me was uncomfortable with the detention because I was also known for being a teacher's pet. In school, I was either a good student or I got away with mischief. So when Goodey forgave us all, he had saved my reputation. I could keep my clean record of having no detention in high school.

*

At lunch time, our food was prepared in the school dining hall. We would assemble at our tables and chat among ourselves until someone banged the table really loud to signal that a prayer was about to take place. We rose from our seats and the whole dining hall would go quiet. One of the school prefects would pray in Latin and then we would sit down and eat. This custom of praying in Latin is something I also practiced at home during vacation. When my parents asked me to say grace, I broke out my Latin, partly showing off and partly because it was the only prayer I knew well. I always began with the word, "Oremus" meaning "Let us pray." By the time I finished praying in

Latin, everyone at the table would smile. No one knew what the prayer meant, but sometimes my father started a slow clap. His daughter had discovered a way to interact with God in Latin. Something he said his mother was also good at. To my father, this was endearing because I was showing more traits that resembled my bad-ass grandmother. And, sometimes, I even imagined her praying in Latin while smoking, coughing out some words accompanied by smoke after each drag from her cigarette.

We spoke more British than American English, using words like "pupil" instead of "student," "break time" instead of "recess," "term" instead of "semester," and we played British sports like badminton, rugby, and netball, which sparked my athleticism. I spent a lot of time at the school pavilion because sports made me feel alive. It also reminded me of playing with the boys in my neighborhood in Sunny Side. Almost every term, I was the captain of a sports team. The only games I wasn't good at were tennis and volleyball. I wasn't terrible at them, but I couldn't master them as well as netball, basketball, and badminton. At K.A., the boys were similar to the ones in my neighborhood. They either liked that I was ruthless at sports or they did everything they could to make me feel awkward about my skills. Once, the boys and girls had to participate in an exercise called The Beep Test. It involved running from one side of the soccer field to the other after the sound of a beep. The sound came from our coach's car, which was parked a few feet from us with the volume on blast. Beep, we ran. Beep, we ran. Beep, we ran. After each interval, the beeps got faster and faster, leaving no time to catch our breath. If you failed to make the timing of the beeps, you could surrender and walk off the field. On this particular day, the sun was out and the field was almost empty. Three out of thirty students kept running and I was one of them. We were down to two boys and one girl. My legs were exhausted, I was sweating profusely and I could barely catch my breath. At first, the girls and some of the boys cheered me on. But when the last boy and me were left running, some of the boys started jeering:

"Ah-ah, Carol, that's enough! You are not a boy!" some said.

"You're making us look bad. *Watopa basi!*" another said, advising me to get tired.

Once the boy I was running with surrendered, all I could hear were cusses and clucks. Mostly words that questioned my femininity: how I ran like a boy, how I was showing off by trying hard, how some boys would never ask me out on a date. It seemed as if the more I ran and did well in sports, the less female I was becoming, the less attractive. And that afternoon, as I ran alone on the soccer field, with my coach and a few girls applauding me, I will never forget how I stopped not because I couldn't run anymore, but because I was afraid to be strong in front of the boys.

"Shakespeare Taught Me English"

I was never the best high school student in the class, but I was a memorable one. I was in my early teens and English was a difficult subject for me to master when it came to writing. It seemed every time I wrote an essay or poetry or answered questions for a test, my English was not clear or coherent. Yet, one author stood out to me when I studied literature in Mrs. Chimombo's class—William Shakespeare. Although I failed English composition a lot, literature was another story in my journey with writing.

It occurred to me when I was placed in the bottom set of English classes, that I secretly liked literature. I was in a class of approximately fifteen students. All of us struggled to understand grammar and how to form a proper complete sentence. The classroom was a square shape with brown desks and chairs aligned against the walls. There were four desks at the center and I sat in the middle with my friends. Whenever our teacher asked us to read, my heart raced with excitement. I wanted to read. I wanted people to hear me change my vocal inflection in order to capture the essence of characters. Before Shakespeare, we read stories like *Death of a Salesman* or we read poetry, which also led to contests I enjoyed. Everyone knew I was the kind of girl who would risk looking like a fool in literature class, but I was also the kind of girl who wanted to be seen as "too cool" for literature.

Most of my friends thought English literature was silly, irrelevant to their lives. And for a while I pretended that it was, indeed, useless. It was well-known that subjects like Biology, Chemistry, and Physics were for smart students who would become something one day. Because of the Malawian obsession with students becoming doctors or scientists, English was a joke, a subject for less ambitious people. I spoke about English the way my father spoke about acting—emphasizing that it was a complete waste of time. Although I hid my love for literature, I was the kind of girl who also liked Latin and Greek, two other subjects that people thought were useless for future careers. I felt strange with this hidden desire for different languages. Exposing myself as this kind of girl was not an option I wanted to explore because I was already struggling with fitting in with other girls. Admitting to my love for language would only make me seem more different. There were no other girls raving about English, Latin, or Greek, so I settled for my pretense just to gain acceptance. I would pretend I didn't want to read, mostly through facial expressions. I trained myself to look bored, aggravated and unenthusiastic. I pretended I didn't like reciting poems. This pretense was tough because when I hit center stage in class, when I had an audience, my passion for poetry was very visible. My smile grew too wide, my voice was too excited and lively for a person who hated literature. Sometimes, I skipped English class with my friends, but instead of enjoying my self-given free time, I would daydream about what I was missing in class, I wondered who was reading out loud or making the class laugh instead of me.

As time went on, I realized I felt the most alive when I used my imagination to bring characters to life, when I stood up to recite my poems in front of the class. It was another opportunity to shine like an actress. I liked having everybody's attention, the thought of them watching me be good at something that was supposedly bad. *Maybe I could convince them to like it too*, I often thought. When asked to read aloud in front of others, I made sure I read, ahead of time, the words of the characters I was assigned. I would imagine what the characters sounded like. I figured out their mood, tone, and intentions. When it was my turn to read, it came out effortlessly sometimes, but other times, my anxiety with the English language took over my efforts to make words flow out of me fluidly. Hearing myself choke up when reading was the worst feeling. Awkward pauses made me feel dumb. It meant I was a student who couldn't read—period.

Shakespeare became the phenomenon that influenced not only how I viewed the English language but how I viewed the world and my writing. In Mrs. Chimombo's class, I was asked to read the role of Bassanio from Shakespeare's *The Merchant of Venice*. I think Mrs. Chimombo could sense that I was secretly passionate about English. It was in the way she smiled at me through her round glasses when I read or spoke in class. Her face would flash red with her head tilted to the side, nodding at me like a proud mother looking at her genius child. But how could that be true if I was in the bottom set of English classes?

Although her supportive nature made me feel good, sometimes, if I read terribly, I gave her stares tinged with doubt and disbelief in her affirmations. Yet, Mrs. Chimombo never stopped asking me to read major roles. I liked it, but my face had to show otherwise. When reading Bassanio, my nerves clawed at my comfort. I wrestled through the lines, still managing to use vocal inflection to bring the character to life. I even expressed myself with a male tone, which always made the class laugh. What my peers didn't know is that it allowed me to dive deeper into gender just as I did when I performed on stage. When we discussed the text, I would express how I enjoyed Shakespeare's creativity and his understanding of human imperfections. Bassanio's challenge to select a gold, silver, or lead casket also showed me how you can't judge a book by its cover. He won a fair lady by humbling himself, by seeing beyond things that are coated in silver and gold. I liked reading him voyeuristically. I liked transforming myself in an imaginative world and being able to face my fear with the English language.

During my spare time, I revisited my Shakespeare texts. I would brush my hand against the textbook as if it were some sacred scroll with hidden truths about life. Then I analyzed each sentence like a puzzle. At first, the structure of the sentences seemed jumbled up, but as I read more and more, my mind rearranged words from early to late modern English. I searched for the subject, verb, and object agreement. Then I looked for what I called the excess baggage of a sentence and separated it with commas. I decoded his thous, thees, and thines, making sure I knew which one was subjective and which one was objective.

Reading Shakespeare made sense to me, but writing my own sentences was still a problem.

Failing English Cambridge IGCSEs came as a blow. When I took the exam, I was so sure I had tried my best when writing my essay response. All I needed was a C-grade in order to pass. When my father showed me the school report, seeing a D broke my heart because I loved a subject I wasn't good at. Seeing a D made me think I would never be able to write anything decent. This bruised my self-esteem in what I write. After my senior year at K.A., I had to return to retake the exam. It was a chance to do better if I wanted to transfer my credits for college. And American colleges were not going to accept someone who couldn't write English.

I passed with a C average. And even though it wasn't a higher grade, which I had wished for, I was grateful for a passing grade. At this stage in my life, I had no idea how crucial English composition and literature would be in my life. No clue that I would be a better writer than I was at that time. No clue that I would perform many Shakespearean roles, that I would major in his studies. Writing about literature I loved strengthened my composition skills. And, today, when people ask me how I speak and write so well, I tell them that "Shakespeare taught me English." It sounds like a joke at first, but that statement couldn't be more accurate and truer for my experience with the English language and writing.

I Appreciate

I was creeping in our corridor again, listening to the loud Tupac Shakur music that was booming from my brothers' room. A sixteen-year-old Charles was rapping lyrics that sounded like a rant. He did it mostly verbatim, sometimes skipping words between beats. I knew some songs by Tupac because of Charles, but not well enough to purchase my own cassette or to listen to his songs alone. Most Malawians knew that Tupac's lyrics had a lot of profanity, but some young people adored him for his talents. He had an ability to express raw honesty about hard American lives in powerful, poetic language laced with vulgar, uncomfortable words like "fuck." Others hated Tupac because of another talented hip-hop artist named Notorious B.I.G., also known as Biggie Smalls. The East Coast-West Coast hip hop rivalry in America, which involved rappers dissing each other on record tracks, had spread across the ocean, reaching Malawian fans. People even chose sides. Tupac's reputation for producing music with profanity kept my interest in him at bay because well-behaved Catholic girls did not indulge in sinful songs. Music with profanity was forbidden in the Kautsire household. My father did not like loud music or any loud noises for that matter. The man turned into the Incredible Hulk with only the bang of a slammed door. But when our parents were not at home, my brothers and I played any music we liked. We even cranked the volume high.

I cracked the bedroom door open, slowly sliding my head into the room, my skinny ten-year-old body next, hoping Charles wouldn't detect an intruder barging in on his rap session. *Please don't tell me to get out*, I thought. He was alone in the room, laying on his bed, playing his Nintendo Game Boy. I watched him for a few seconds as he bopped his head and sometimes waved one hand in the air, making a gangster sign as he sang in unison with Tupac. His head popped up from his video game, probably from the peripheral sight of my bright periwinkle t-shirt and blue jeans. He glanced at me, then his right hand flew up making another gangster sign, some fingers bent, others stuck out, waving to the rhythm of the song. I didn't know what it meant. While he was still looking at me, he rapped the words that came from his stereo.

"You try to trap me say you pregnant and guess who the daddy, don't wanna fall for it!" He laughed.

I stopped at the door and smiled. Charles was notorious for randomly blurting out music lyrics to people around him, if he felt like it.

"Come in!" he yelled over the music, his head still bopping to the tune.

I ran to his bed and planted myself at the edge, near his feet. He was still rapping in a lower voice. I listened, wishing I knew the words too, in awe of how he could memorize and recite the lyrics to so many songs. I listened but couldn't understand a word Tupac was saying. *Thank*

God I don't listen to this guy's music. The chorus was better. The lady sang slower: It sounded like a song with a good message, but I still wondered about who trapped whom with pregnancy. I watched Charles as he continued playing his Game Boy. His fingers were moving so fast. I was curious to know which game he had mastered. I figured maybe if I stuck around longer, he would get tired and let me play and I could beat whatever level he was on. This worked sometimes. I waited, listening to more Tupac until the song ended. Then, a brief silence. Another song would soon begin. When it did, I couldn't make out the first few words, but it sounded like Tupac was in mid-conversation with someone. Then, a deep, loud voice swearing. An avalanche of "fucks."

My eyes popped. Charles was now lip-syncing the words. When I heard the beat, I recognized the song, *Hit Em Up*. My high school girlfriends and I knew how much boys loved the song, but we decided that it was terrible because of the high levels of profanity. I didn't have much of an opinion about music I hadn't listened to, but going along with this judgment helped me fit in with everyone. The girls and I made it a point to dislike this specific song. My first instinct was to run out of the room, not only because of my allegiance to the girls at school but to remove any chances of Charles chasing me out because of profanity. He and Trevor always blocked my eyes and ears if there was any vulgarity around me. But on this day, Charles wasn't fazed. At ten years old, I had two theories—either he was distracted by his video game or this was a new sign that having me around vulgar things didn't bother him anymore. After all, we both went to Kamuzu Academy, where most kids listened to artists like Tupac, Biggie, and Snoop Dogg. We even danced to their music at school discos and variety shows. So I suspect he didn't think it made a difference if he prevented his little sister from listening to music she was likely to listen to when he wasn't around. True, but not in the case of some Tupac songs. My brother's calm triggered a challenging spirit in me. If Charles could handle this music, then I could too. I stayed and listened to the forbidden song.

Tupac was pissed, and the fast words that flowed out of him blazed with insults. I tried to follow the narrative to *Hit Em Up,* but all I got were fragments of who, what, when, where and why. I listened for recurring people and places—West side, Bad Boy, Puffy, Biggie Smalls, Junior M.A.F.I.A., Lil Caesar, Mobb Deep, Lil Kim (I was most familiar with Lil Kim). I noticed how he addressed people rudely. I pieced together common references to what was happening—making claims, guns, prison—the highlight being people getting killed. He insulted people in many different ways. I listened to a sea of murderous words, a crash course on Tupac's rage.

By the time the song had ended, I was standing at the edge of Charles's bed. I had been wiggling my body around because of my discomfort with the lyrics—gasping, sighing, popping my eyes at words that overwhelmed me. Sometimes I cackled, thrilled about partaking in mischief by listening to all the "fucks" in the song. No wonder why some people thought Tupac's music was of the devil. The song was loaded with violence and disrespect. Yet, in the midst of all the hostile language, I was happy that I had finally listened to it. Two thoughts swirled in my mind.

One: maybe people were allowed to speak this way in America. This could have been what separated Malawians from Americans. *They* had freedom of speech and *we*, Malawians, were silenced by our traditions and culture, suffocating in our own judgments about liberated people like Tupac. But I hoped that freedom of expression was now emerging for Malawians but in the right context. I never liked hearing boys in Malawi refer to each other as "niggaz" and it was meant to be hip. It was as if America was colonizing us through television and radio, but I always felt there needed to be boundaries in language that shouldn't be crossed. There was nothing to rejoice about in profanity but I liked the idea of freedom of speech. Two: maybe girls were too closed-minded, mentally and emotionally unfit to handle harsh words about hard lives in America. With my obsession about being tough, listening to Tupac would put me in the rank of a girl who was psychologically fit and fully awakened to American culture. Or better yet, the fact that Charles wasn't bothered that I listened to Tupac meant he saw me as someone mature enough to handle it. I took joy in these thoughts. That day, I focused on how passionate Tupac sounded in his rage and was mesmerized by his boldness, the fire in his language. I walked over to the stereo and lowered the volume, still skeptical about Charles being okay with my presence.

"Tcha, what was that other song you were listening to?" I asked, pretending *Hit Em Up* didn't play, in case he planned on chasing me out the next time it played.

"*Do for Love*," he said, barely looking up from his Game Boy.

"And what were those words you sang when I walked in?"

He lifted his head and rapped the words very fast, "You try to trap me say you pregnant and guess who the daddy / don't wanna fall for it!" He laughed again. He sounded triumphant.

"What's so funny about that?" I asked. I wanted in on the joke.

"Because the guy figured her out. She wanted him to stay, but the baby wasn't his," he said, explaining as if I knew the whole story. He sounded like one of my friends when they badly described a sitcom no one knew about.

My face was blank. I still didn't understand why it was funny to him. But I had my suspicion that Charles imagined his own sitcoms in his head and that's why he randomly sang lyrics to people. Maybe somewhere in his mind, he caught a woman trying to trap *him* by lying or faking a pregnancy. In an imagined world, Charles was a sixteen-year-old Malawian boy with "baby daddy" issues. But I still retained the lyrics in my memory because when Charles had said them, the rhythm of the words was catchy. I decided that I wanted to rap like Tupac.

For days, I snuck into my brothers' room when they weren't around. I sat on the floor next to the stereo, a notebook and pen in hand. I listened to *Do for Love*. Stopping, rewinding and playing the song over and over again until I had written all the lyrics in my notebook. I also enjoyed another song called *Dear Mama*. It illustrated not only Tupac's mastery of words but how perceptive he was about his own flawed life, about humanity. In *Do for Love*, he sang about relationship struggles, how someone could be relentless to stay in a toxic relationship because of love. To Tupac, love wasn't a simple on-off switch you flicked depending on whether or not someone was good for you. He understood the complications, the different degrees and shades of love that people feel when they do what they can to stay together. As the lyrics state, "You tried everything, but you don't give up."

Tupac and I had something in common. This became evident in the song, *Dear Mama*. We both loved our mothers. He laid out his heart on that track, showing his appreciation for his mother's love, how she was honest with him, how she disciplined and provided for him in tough circumstances, loving him even when he was up to no good in the streets. He gives vivid descriptions of his difficult past—growing up with a missing father, being poor, seeing his mother in jail, being in constant trouble with the police and starting a thug life not only because he needed money, but because "even though they [thugs] sold drugs / They showed a young brother love." Tupac knew the pressures of life that made people pursue dangerous choices. His message to his mother was that he may not be able to pay her back for all she did but that his plan (even writing the song itself) was to show her that he understood what she went through to raise him. Tupac had compassion, and the more I listened to his songs, the more I realized that he wasn't just a man with an agenda to glorify violence or other kinds of criminal behavior. If he sounded like a rabble-rouser in songs like *Hit Em Up*, I assumed he was driven by hurt and rage like any other person. I understood that the same compassionate and perceptive Tupac had another side that was confrontational if he felt wronged. And I could relate.

Before I could shock my girlfriends with my new passion for rap music, before I could unleash words by the Tupac we had dubbed devilish, I decided to test my vocals on my father. I had memorized the lyrics for both *Do for Love* and *Dear Mama*, and I had convinced myself that the songs were decent enough for my father to approve. He would be impressed with my rap skills and, maybe, if he were attentive to the lyrics, he would realize that his daughter is very wise. My mission came to pass on a regular Saturday afternoon when my father asked me to accompany him to buy vegetables at the market. I was sitting in the kitchen, sulking, as my mother showed me how to cook beef stew. She was standing at the sink, cutting cow meat into small pieces. I had refused to do the cutting because I told my mother I wanted to keep all my fingers, to which she replied that the American actor, Jensen Ackles, for whom I had declared my love throughout the house, would never marry a woman who doesn't know how to cut meat. So I sulked, not because of my fear of cutting meat, but the thought of Jensen Ackles refusing to marry me. My father walked into the kitchen.

"Put your shoes on. Let's go to Limbe market," he said.

I jumped up from the chair, relieved that my father was rescuing me from kitchen chores. I ran to my bedroom and grabbed my sneakers, then snuck into my brother's room to steal the Tupac cassette. I lowered the volume on the stereo and cued up *Do for Love*. My father sounded the car horn. I dashed back to the kitchen, out the door and into my father's

Peugeot 605. When I shut the car door, I immediately reached for the radio.

"Ah-ah! Buckle your seatbelt," my father said.

I buckled up, then resumed my desperate reach for the eject button on the car radio. I removed the cassette that was inside. Time to take a break from our usual Indian music jam sessions. My father also tried to make me listen to classical music whenever we went on car rides— Tchaikovsky, Bach, Beethoven, and Mozart—but I thought music without lyrics was boring. The only exception was if I heard it in cartoons like *Tom and Jerry* or *Looney Tunes*. I slipped in the Tupac cassette as my father reversed the car away from the garage. It was excellent timing. You would think my father and I were in a movie and the music was the perfectly cued background to our lives. I grinned, while bopping my head to the subtle introductory beat of *Do for Love,* excited that I was safely reeling my father into the world of rap with a Tupac song that had no profanity.

I started rapping.

I was waving indiscernible gang signs with my little fingers. They probably didn't mean anything because all I did was bend different fingers as I had seen Charles do in his room. I waved to the rhythm of Tupac's song and all that mattered was keeping up with the beat. Words poured out of my mouth, but I barely looked at my father. I did, however, try to see his reaction in my peripheral vision. He had one hand on the steering wheel and the other held a cigarette, elbow on the edge of the car window so the smoke could diffuse outside. Then, the song came to the second verse, the one with a catchy line. I was ready to muster up a tough look while I said it—arms set to make hard waves, fingers ready to gesture what I didn't know were a sign of devil horns, vocals ready to punch the words with force. I shouted louder than the other lyrics I had sung. "You try to trap me say you pregnant and guess who the daddy / don't wanna fall for it!" I smiled triumphantly just like Charles, continuing in a lower voice with the rest of the lyrics.

You would think I was accusing my father of something. He was now looking at me. I knew I had sparked his attention. So I rapped my words more intently as if I was schooling my father with Tupac's concerns about hit-and-run relationships, cheating, happiness, and companionship. He was listening because although he was paying attention to the road, I saw his head turn to me from time to time. I even saw him grinning, but I wasn't sure if it was because of my rap skills or the fact that I was dabbling with the depth of Tupac's message about love. When the song ended, I lowered the volume because I knew *Hit Em Up* was next on the tape. There was no way I would allow my father to be hit in the face with profanity like I had been in my brother's room. I pressed forward on the radio. My father chuckled.

"Who is this rapper?" he asked.

"Tupac," I said, "Charles listens to him too" as if the mention of my brother guaranteed my father's approval of the song.

"*Nde,* you can sing," he said, almost making fun of me.

"It's a good song and people misunderstand Tupac. Rap isn't just about swearing," I explained defensively.

"I see," he said. Then silence.

I played the cassette in a low volume to cue up the song, *Dear Mama*. If Tupac swore, at least it wouldn't blast through the whole car. I would also explain that sometimes he swears but that it is an American thing—freedom of expression.

"If you could memorize your school work the way you've memorized this song, I would be happy," he said.

"But I can do both. I learn from books *and* music," I insisted.

"No. These rap songs are just personal arguments people have. School is something else."

I wanted him to explain further, but I knew I would be arguing with a man who had already made up his mind that rap wasn't something his daughter could learn from. But how would I begin explaining it, if he ever happened to listen to a song like *Hit Em Up*? If anything, it would prove his point that all I was being exposed to were heated arguments about personal misunderstandings.

"Put back the tape you found in the radio. I want to teach you something," he said.

I stopped forwarding the tape. For a second, I wanted to say, "But I want to teach *you* something about Tupac," that there was another song that talks about Tupac's appreciation for his mother. I wanted to say Tupac knew his bad behavior was unacceptable but that life had also weighed heavily on him and that he understood the love of a parent who had taken care of him in hard circumstances.

Upset, I switched the tapes, vigorously pulling out the Tupac cassette and slamming my father's inside—something I knew he hated.

"*Bwino*! Be careful with that."

"Sorry," I said, frowning. I looked out the window.

We were passing a cream-colored brick building, Malawi College of Medicine. A few shirtless boys were playing basketball on the courts next to it. *I bet if I played Tupac for them, they would appreciate his music.* Classical music had been playing for a few seconds since I had slipped in my father's tape; but now, the music was building up to something. My heart began to beat at an odd pace, as if the sounds were seducing me, against my will, to listen to their suspenseful notes. My imagination had taken flight before I became aware of it. First the sound of trumpets, announcing something to come as if we were in a King's court. Then, marching drums, a band of hundreds of people. Then, cannons went off. Sometimes I thought they were fireworks. Then, the sound of something flying in the air, or was it dropping from the sky? Whatever it was sounded like something drawing closer to my imagined crowd. Then, clanging church bells rang out against a spiraling tune that grew more and more pronounced, creating suspense for what would happen next. Then, a playful tune, like circus music, almost out of place amid the serious notes of the tune. Then, cannons went off again, the circus music now underscored the explosions. This time I was sure they were cannons and not fireworks because the explosions were very distinct, more violent than celebratory fireworks. Then, everything went in reverse order—the clanging bells returned, a swift rushing sound of resolution in the drums, trumpets. Then silence. My heart, still racing.

That was my father's lesson.

Tchaikovsky's 1812 Overture. My father and I called it "Tchelowaski," a word that only mimicked the phonetics of his name and which we used because pronouncing Tchaikovsky was difficult. By the time we arrived at the Limbe market, my father had explained that he loved classical music because it made him exercise his imagination.

"Ms. Kautsire, classical music tells stories," he said, "And you have to use the sounds to determine if it is about happiness, war, nature, love—you name it."

"Like Tupac's music," I jumped in, still making a case for Tupac's talent and perceptiveness.

"In a way, yes," he said. His tone was skeptical, but a "yes" was enough for me.

All I wanted was for my father to realize that life's lessons came from any type of music, which I'm sure he knew. But I was adamant about removing society's dismissal of rap music as inappropriate devilish music. Such outlooks denied talent. I also wanted my father to know that I was a girl who was mentally and emotionally strong enough to sift through hard language about harsh realities. I imagined it would frighten my father to witness his little girl praising rap music by a man who was considered a thug. But I was that kind of girl—a girl who, despite the profanity and violence in Tupac's raging lyrics, had been won over by his honesty, his understanding of the human condition, and his compassion. His mastery of words reminded me of Shakespeare.

"Dad, may I please play one more Tupac song on our way home?" I asked before exiting the car.

"Sure," he said, a playful wince in his smile, "One more is fine."

"Okay. Because I have something to teach you too," I said, finally, smiling like a child setting a booby trap. And where better to begin schooling my father on Tupac than with a song about a parent's love for a child who got in a lot of trouble. Maybe I wasn't always on the run from cops like Tupac and maybe I wasn't roaming around with street thugs, but I had caused enough problems for my parents to wonder if I recognized and respected their love despite my mischievous ways. My rap lesson to my father was my plan to show him what I understood about love, the bond between parent and child. Through Tupac's *Dear Mama,* I would express how much I appreciated him and my mother.

Jousting With Nuns

A ten-year-old demon. The Catholic nuns must have thought I was one when I argued with them about the proper behavior of young girls. My parents were members of Saint Montfort Catholic Church in Blantyre City, and each year, the nuns organized a weekend female grooming event where they taught girls how to behave. Most girls who attended the event were from lower or middle-class families. I forget how much it cost in Malawian Kwachas, but my father said it amounted to something less than one American dollar. The nuns taught things that would help us understand what girls communicate when interacting with others and we would learn how to distinguish ourselves from boys. They covered body language, speech, fashion, menstruation, romantic relationships, and lots about sex. The verbal jousting began when we were informed about God's opinion on female etiquette, and the battle grew worse by the time we covered how body language led to incest.

*

My mother dropped me off behind the church, where there were long rectangular brick buildings and classrooms with no chairs inside. Some windows were shattered and all the blue doors were covered in dirt. There were two nuns with clipboards at the doorway of each classroom, all of them wearing blue habits with white wimples. About forty to fifty girls my age carried their belongings into the classrooms as the nuns checked off names on their lists. I was ready to scream and bolt for my escape when my mother parked the car by a dirt road next to the building. I immediately noticed that most girls wore dresses and skirts. Then, I looked down at my blue jeans, shook my head and rolled my eyes. My first sign that I was out of place. I had been complaining since we left home because I didn't want to be disciplined like an untrained animal by nuns whose lives looked nothing like what I wanted my life to be.

"Ma, but haven't you already taught me how to behave like a girl?" I whined, leaning my head against the car window in the front passenger seat.

"Yes, but there are some things that other adults have to teach you. The lessons don't come from mothers," she said, "It's similar to *kuvinidwa*," referring to the coming-of-age ceremonies that are held in the villages. Usually, the aunts and grandmothers of the child run the event. The girl sits on the floor at the center of the room, wrapped in a chitenje. Then, the women circle around, teasing and taunting her about her body, teaching her about female etiquette, how to do chores in the domestic area and how to please a man in different ways. They can poke her body, smack her face, push her around a little and be explicitly vulgar about sex. In action, it looks very disrespectful, and it was very uncomfortable to hear and watch. One can understand why mothers aren't part of the ceremony. But these aunts and grandmothers create harsh environments that can make some girls stronger. It's like boot camp, where sergeants yell in your face, targeting vulnerabilities that could make you break into tears in front of others. The roughness is supposed to make you tough. I had heard my friends and cousins recount how they cried during their ceremonies, how they had to tough it out as their favorite aunts and sweet grandmothers bullied them to be strong.

"But I told you, *Ma*...I don't like these things because I'm learning something else at school," I protested, "I won't go."

After five minutes of my mother trying to convince me to get out of the car, I looked outside the window and there was my friend, Limbikani, arriving with her mother. Limbikani and I were neighborhood friends and we attended South End Primary School together. She was carrying a backpack behind her, a pillow and blanket in her arms, walking calmly towards one of the classrooms. I smiled a little, but hid it from my mother so she wouldn't think I was happy about being there.

"OK, I'll go," I said, opening the car door.

"Good girl!" my mother exclaimed.

I grabbed my stuff from the backseat; a pillow, blanket, and a bag full of clothes, snacks and things for showering. I would later learn that there were no showers. Buckets would be provided, which we filled with cold tap water for bathing. I gave my mother a quick hug and told her not to be late picking me up on Sunday afternoon. Then, I ran to Limbikani. Excitement set in when we connected. We hugged, jumping up and down because the event suddenly felt like a sleepover. We got our names checked on the list and entered a big classroom. About twenty to thirty girls filled the classroom. Each of us set up places to sleep on the cold, cement floor. Limbikani and I found a space near the wall—that way, we could at least lean on something. I had slept on the floor many times before, at my mother's home village in Chikwawa, so the sleeping conditions were not unfamiliar or shocking. Our first class on female behavior would be held on Saturday afternoon after we had cleaned the classrooms as the nuns requested.

At night, the room got stuffy and a mixture of body odor and dirt circulated the room. Mosquitoes had dibs on our young bodies, swarming everywhere like malaria traps. I tried to ignore the smell, swatting mosquitos as they flew near me. The nuns knew exactly who I was because my father was the chairman of many church committees—he was the man who devoted himself to making sure the church had what it needed, especially when it came to financial needs. The nuns had a great deal of respect for him, and a part of me was fearless about causing trouble because I knew they wouldn't cross the daughter of their beloved chairman. But he was also the reason I was there, while I was home from Kamuzu Academy. I was supposed to represent him as proof of his commitment to help the church. I was there so they could fix naughty behaviors and help us to be well-behaved girls.

There was a slim girl with shaved black hair, an oval-shaped head, long eyelashes, and thin lips sitting across from me. Her eyes were fixed on me. I don't remember when I noticed it, but I found myself darting my eyes away from her because she never broke eye contact. It's as if I could feel her looking at my body, analyzing my gestures and facial expressions. When I looked at her, she lit up and smiled as if she knew me from somewhere. Sometimes, she looked shy. A nun was shouting from across the room—something about getting ready for bed. Everybody was preparing for bed. With so much stillness, you could now hear mosquitoes buzzing everywhere. Limbikani was unpacking her stuff from her backpack. The girl with a shaved head walked toward me. She was about 5'5 and wore a dress, a chitenje wrapped around her waist. I could see her looking at me from a peripheral view. When she got closer, I could no longer pretend that I hadn't seen her. She stood beside me and I looked up from where I was sitting.

"Shapu!" she said. Chichewa slang for "What's up."

"Shapu," I said, grinning.

"What's your name?"

"Carol," I stood up. "What's yours?"

"Linda." She smiled.

I nodded, still grinning, but not knowing what to say next or why she was talking to me. We stood in awkward silence, grinning as if one of us had said something interesting. Again, from a peripheral view, I could feel her eyes looking closely at all of me. *What is she looking at?* I thought. Clueless about what she might be thinking too. My body grew tense and I was still nodding my head for no reason.

"You should come and sleep near me tomorrow," she said.

I froze. *Why?* I thought. She probably wanted to be friends. Maybe this was how some girls made friends.

"Okay," I said, not knowing if I meant it.

She smiled. "Sleep well," she said, then walked away.

*

Another stuffy classroom. Only this time, mosquitoes were off duty and flies had taken over the afternoon shift. There were about fifteen of us in one room. The other girls were in classrooms adjacent to the one I was in. The room had long wooden tables, two chairs behind each one. I sat at the front of the classroom next to Limbikani. Our table was right at the center. Limbikani may have been surprised because the Carol she knew in primary school would sit at the back of the classroom like a rebel.

I knew my intentions for the nuns. British and American lifestyles aside, I was ready to give an ear to the traditional ideas the nuns wanted to teach. I was ready to find out what Malawian women saw as decent behavior. My eyes panned the room, looking at the girls around me, chatting and laughing. Some girls had braids, others tiny afros. Most of them had black hair that was chemically relaxed. Mine was relaxed too, tied back in a ponytail and keeping up with Western ideals. I listened to the sound of the girls' voices— their vocal energy when lost in conversation, the occasional high-pitched shrieks and soft chuckles. I observed how their skirts and dresses complemented the shapes of their bodies. Even Limbikani wore a skirt. Their bodies fit well in their clothes, everything seemed to hang right. Something I never felt when I wore skirts and dresses. I was the only one in blue jeans and a t-shirt, a second sign that I was out of place. And when a beautiful, light-skinned, chubby nun walked into the room, the next thing she looked at after making eye contact with me for the first time, was my blue jeans.

I had a mindset that didn't believe anything the nuns said. I mocked them in my head, *you would think the nuns have God on speed dial*, I thought in my rebellion. It was in their surety of expressing what God expected for young girls, what pleased Him and what didn't. My head voices couldn't stop the mockery and disrespect for God: God had a list of demands, which the light-skinned chubby nun enlightened us with, and the specificity of his expectations had a close correspondence with Malawian culture. God wanted us to sit with our legs together or crossed at the ankles. He wanted us to contain the steps of our walk (no giant manly strides), and he wanted us to kneel before our elders to show respect. God didn't allow mini-skirts, tube tops or any outfits that exposed too much skin. An emphasis was placed on how God approved of girls who wore chitenjes (I guess my mother was right). God wanted girls to have soft voices (no loud booming voices. Because God created such loudness for boys). God wanted us to avoid discussing vulgar things, especially anything that had to do with male or female private parts. Breasts were a no-no too. If we were menstruating, God most certainly did not want us discussing our periods with boys. God wasn't too thrilled about tampons and pads either; instead, he wanted us to use rags that we would wash after using. God was into recycling. As for romantic relationships, God thought it was best to wait until we were done with school and ready to start our families. Premarital sex was a sin. This was the darkest sin to avoid. Something about having sex once made you a sinner for life—you couldn't make "amends" for a sin with a broken virginal knot (pun-intended). As I said, I didn't know God well enough to know what he wanted or didn't want, so I resulted in thoughts that were rude and disrespectful to the nuns—something I regret until today.

It is inappropriate for a girl to hug her father and brothers, said the light-skinned, chubby nun; God does not approve of such sexual advances. When I heard this, my mind could no longer contain the questions that swirled around in my head. I looked at the girls behind me, searching for reactions in their faces, trying to detect if anyone else found this rule ridiculous. All the girls were attentive. None seemed stirred in a negative way. I looked at the nun. My hand flew up. She nodded for me to speak.

"Is there a spiritual society that makes these rules?" I asked, in a condescending tone.

She stood silent for a second, made no eye contact with me, then smiled at the class. "No questions," she said.

"Why not?" I asked in a softer tone.

Silence.

She stood still, her eyes fixed on the wall at the back of the classroom. I took this as a sign that I was on to something and that I was uncovering a secret the church was keeping.

"Wouldn't God want me to ask questions if I am confused about his rules?" I continued. "In school, we are always told to ask questions."

"I said, no questions," she repeated.

I looked around, shaking my head. A few girls looked shocked. Some were trying to hold back their laughs. Others were so afraid that they simply looked down at their desks or outside the windows.

The lecture continued. "You can't just throw yourselves into the arms of men. And the same goes for your fathers and brothers. Be careful how you touch them and how they touch you." I knew where this was going. *Old-fashioned adults who think everything is about sex*, I thought. Their rules frustrated me. They struck me as perverts for thinking hugs were sexual advances. Like a rebellious journalist who won't leave without a story, I fired question after question. I even sounded just like my Lieutenant Mother.

"Are you afraid that we will be the kind of girls who sleep with our fathers and brothers?" I snapped. "Because I don't see the problem with hugs. What's the real problem? I hug my father and brothers all the time and none of us want to have sex with each other." My hands were shaking and my heart raced because I knew how rude the question was. But my blood boiled because of my frustration with their teachings, which seemed to suggest that female bodies were sinful plagues that could drive men to incest.

"Did I not say no questions?" she shouted, finally looking at me. Rage illuminated her light-skinned face, which was slowly turning red.

A few girls laughed. Some gasped. "Shaaa! But this girl is crazy," someone whispered. The nun walked outside the classroom. The room got noisy. We all exchanged looks, wondering where she was going or what would happen next. Limbikani smiled at me. "But *Carol…*" she began, then went silent. She looked as if she was ready to melt or vanish into thin air to avoid being seen next to me. Then, we heard talking outside. A few seconds later, another nun followed the one I had aggravated. Both looked directly at me. The other nun was short and slim and had a darker skin tone. There was something quiet yet stern about her. When she stood in front of my table, she leaned in.

"Carol, I am told you are disturbing the class. Can you please save your questions for later?" she said.

"If this is a class, shouldn't we ask questions?"

"Yes, but first you must learn what is expected of you."

"But I don't agree with everything," I said, defiantly, almost laughing at how mediocre our dialogue sounded, thinking myself smarter than the nun. Once again, I was channeling my grandmother's stubbornness.

"Okay," she said, readjusting herself to a firm posture, "Ask then."

The classroom fell silent. The girls looked as if they were holding their breath. I thought of how disappointed my parents would be if they heard about my behavior, but I had too much adrenaline to stop myself.

"Why can't we hug our fathers?"

"Because you can't just allow men to touch your body."

"But they are our *fathers*!" I protested, thinking it should be common sense that fathers don't sleep with daughters.

"Yes. But they are *men*," she said.

"So we'll go to hell for hugging them?"

"Hugging can lead to sinful behavior, yes."

"Because our hugs will make our brothers and fathers want to have sex with us." I mocked the idea, again, with a condescending tone. The girls laughed. High-fives all around the room. Some cheered my name, "Kalo!" I didn't know any of their names, but I smiled at everyone.

"That's enough!" The light-skinned nun shouted from the door.

The nuns, who were now looking at each other, were probably thinking of what to do to restore order. Both walked outside of the classroom. The class went wild, shouting questions that ranged from curiosity to harsh offensive banter. We laughed while we were at it. If anything, we had created Pandemonium—hell was empty and all the devils were in that classroom.

There was no punishment for our behavior, which surprised me. I still wonder if it was because the wild protests were initiated by the daughter of a chairman of a significant church committee. Were they afraid that I would report their cautions on incest to my father? Or did the nuns secretly agree that asking questions was important in a classroom? And that maybe they never prepared for a situation where girls questioned what they taught? In retrospect, I realize that they were warning us about men who may not have sexual boundaries within their families. They were teaching us that incest can happen to anyone and that if we were careful with how we behaved around men, nobody would be seduced by our bodies in the first place. Yet, their lesson on incestuous hugs was muddied by framing it as God's specific command—that a hug was a definite trigger for sexual attraction. It wasn't wrong for us to ask questions either. However, I admit that we were wrong for spewing vulgar remarks at the nuns. We probably should have been punished. After all, as one nun said the day we had arrived, we were there to learn to avoid rowdy unladylike behavior like the kind we had displayed in the classroom. This was an early childhood opportunity to learn discipline.

*

That night, I slept next to Linda, the girl with a shaved head. Limbikani and I had decided to relocate from our sleeping area after enjoying a humorous conversation with Linda. It turned out she liked clowning too and she introduced us to all her friends. She had many at the event, and most of them were fond of her shy-appearing, yet daring personality. I laid on the floor with my back to her and wrapped my body in my brown blanket. I wore soft cotton pajamas and did everything to keep the cold floor from touching my skin. The room was dark and mosquitoes were out for blood. After slapping a few from my face, I slowly began to doze off. But just before I could fall completely asleep, I was woken by something behind me. It was fiddling with my blanket. A snake—that was my first thought. I was scared of them. And my heart raced at the thought of a black mamba wrapping itself around me. I thought of jumping up but what if I stepped on it in the dark, provoking its venomous bite? I stayed still, closing my eyes tight, as if shutting them harder could make the snake disappear. My blanket came loose from its tight wrap. Something slid in. A hand. Cold against the skin around my waist. I did not move at all. I did not open my eyes. I knew who it was, and I had heard of girls who liked other girls. In Malawi, nobody spoke about same-sex attraction. It was a strange subject, and I didn't know what to think of it. But I wonder, now, what the nuns would have said about this.

Late Bloomer

My body took too long to mature. I was considered a late bloomer in high school—well, at least in comparison to other girls in my class. When I started high school at Kamuzu Academy, I was one of the youngest girls in my cohort. Most of them were two to three years older than me. Since I was only nine years old, I had a flat chest, flat backside, no hair on my arms and legs and many girls inevitably got their periods before me. This aggravated me because in high school, having none of these things meant I was still a child who couldn't groom herself. I was not yet exhibiting mature or attractive qualities, which most teenage girls hoped for.

I never paid close attention to my body until I started becoming interested in boys. High school is where the shape of my body really counted when it came to creating attraction. My friends and I often spoke about what it meant to grow up. And before we got to how boys liked big breasts and butts, we discussed what it meant for our bodies to transform and mature. We came to a few conclusions. Having big breasts and a big butt meant you were blooming into an attractive girl. Having hair on your legs meant you had reached the age where you could start cultivating beauty practices, all heavily influenced by European standards. Shaving was a sign that you were responsible, keeping up with society's beauty expectations, as a proper young lady. Getting your period meant you were ready to have sex, that boys could admire you in sexual ways. After all, your body would be screaming to get knocked up. The flip side was that since we were still young and in high school, we were expected to hush our hormones and keep our legs closed.

I wasn't the kind of girl who stuffed socks in a bra to pretend I had breasts, but I was the kind of girl who faked shaving my legs as though I had hair. Each Saturday morning, my friends would gather their shaving sticks, soaps, creams, and towels and shave by the cement sinks outside our dorm rooms, where we washed laundry with our bare hands. Some carried pails of water and sat by the lawn outside their bedrooms. I watched them roll up their jeans, wet and soap their legs. Sometimes I couldn't see the hair on their legs at all. They gently shaved off their hairs, looking closely at their skin, letting the shaving stick slide smoothly up their legs as if they were sculpting art. They did this while chatting, recounting the hottest gossip—usually about relationships, budding flings, singling out who had sex with whom in the squash courts—and lots of laughing. Everyone looked so happy shaving. I felt left out. Sometimes, someone said something to me as I watched enviously on the side.

"O! Carol, you have no hair on your legs!" "O! Shame, too bad!" they would say.

I hated showing my legs and I tried to cover them as often as I could. I wore jeans all the time and got into the habit of covering them with a blanket or chitenje if I was sitting on a chair or my bed. I had very smooth legs, a smoothness that my friends were striving for. But since I wasn't shaving, I never cared for the fact that my legs were already smooth. I was more worried that I was still a child in my friends' eyes. What triggered my crazy notion to pretend to shave the hair on my legs was not hair-related. There was talk about not having my period, as well as my lack of breasts and a big backside.

The boys in my class often teased girls about being on the rag. Once, my friend, Kevin, who was two years older than me, told me he could sense when a girl was on her period by feeling her wrists. Something about the warmth of the hand, he said. We were seated in our chairs in chemistry class, waiting for our teacher to begin his lecture, when Kevin slid his arms towards mine on the wooden desk.

"Do you bleed?" Kevin asked, feeling my wrist with his fingers.

I pulled my hand away. "Stop it," I whispered, smiling but embarrassed.

"You don't look like you bleed," he concluded.

His eyes looked as if his assessment of me had dulled his day. He turned his body to face the front of the class, as if it was a waste of time to talk to a girl who hadn't gotten her period yet. I ignored him. But my heart raced at the fact that he could tell I didn't menstruate just by looking at me. Kevin was a very observant boy and often shared his philosophies about life, love, and other existential subjects. I panicked that his wisdom might have enabled him to see my body through my clothes. After that exchange, I felt naked around boys. When I interacted with them, I tightened my body and fidgeted a lot, mostly hunching my

140

shoulders, placing books or anything I could find in front of me to hide in plain sight. I also observed carefully how they looked at me, tracing where their eyes would land on my body, wondering if they could see my nakedness, my hairless skinny body with a flat chest, no butt—wondering if I appalled them.

I was twelve years old when I started faking my period and shaving my hairless legs. I had already purchased a pink shaving stick before I left home to start the new school year. When my mother and I went shopping for food and things I would need for boarding school, I spontaneously threw the shaving stick in the shopping cart. My mother never asked me about it when the cashier rang it up at the checkout line. Maybe she didn't see it. But if she noticed, it did not surprise me that she didn't ask. At this point, we had not yet discussed shaving or menstruation.

The thought of faking a shave was born months before the Saturday morning when I followed my roommate, Mia, to the cement sinks where we washed our laundry. I had wanted to join the other girls for so long that I finally grabbed my new shaving stick, soap and wrapped a towel over my shorts and around my waist.

"Which sink do you want?" Mia asked, clueless of my deception.

"The one on the left," I said, pointing at the one farthest away from people who would pass by.

I hesitated to move for a second and watched Mia instead. She climbed up the cement sink, sat on the side of it and placed her legs under the tap. She began the process— wet legs, apply soap, then gently slide the stick against legs. I was attentive. *Don't forget to do it with grace. People who shave look happy.* I climbed up and followed Mia's steps—wet legs, apply soap, but when I looked at the blade of the shaving stick, fear froze me. *What if I cut myself?* But I was already sitting by the sink with soaped legs, Mia would question my hesitation. I had to commit to my pretense. Mia was now in her own rhythm, sliding the stick up her leg and rinsing it after every stroke. *Slide and rinse, slide and rinse*, I took in the motion I would mimic. Looking closely at my soaped bare legs, I placed the blade on the skin of my right leg—a very slight touch—then I slowly slid the stick up. The blade scraped my skin. I stopped mid-slide to check for blood. Nothing. I continued. The slide-and-stops went on for a while, hoping Mia wouldn't turn to her left to look at my awkward shaving.

"Wow, *Mesho*, I grew so much hair," she said at one point, "Nasty!" *Mesho* is an endearing Chichewa slang meaning "roommate," or "roomie" to be more precise.

"Mine aren't so bad," I said.

My *Mesho* and I didn't talk about the hottest gossip. We weren't laughing. And I most certainly did not look like I was sculpting art. We shaved in silence—Mia, performing her flawless rhythm. Me, checking for blood every few seconds. When she washed her legs to finish, I quickly rinsed off mine too. I don't think I shaved much. I didn't even get to my left leg before we returned to our room. My shaving pretense was a success. I was ready to fake bleeding.

*

I did it on a normal school day. It was early in the morning, when the night was slowly giving way to daylight. I knocked on my friend's bedroom door and asked for a pad. Her name was Alinafe. She usually looked out for me on campus, the big sister I never had. Asking Mia was out of the question because I wasn't sure how many of my body issues she was keeping track of. Tampons were also out of the question. Catholic nuns had warned me about them, and I had also heard some girls talk about potentially breaking their virginity from cotton penetration. I believed this myth.

"I finally started my period today," I told Alinafe.

"Welcome to the club, *Mwanii*!" she said, excited for me. *Mwanii* was one of my many high school nicknames. It means "kiddo." She got up from her bed and fetched a pad in her locker. In no time, she yanked out a thick white pad. "Do you know how to use it?"

"No," I said, shaking my head, feeling shy. Seeing the pad made my lie feel real.

Alinafe explained how to peel the papers on the pad, how to place it at the center of my underwear, reminding me to check it after an hour or two, to make sure it doesn't overflow.

"Sometimes your period can be heavy, so don't forget to keep checking it," she said.

"I won't."

"Here's another one for later." She handed me a second pad. I walked out of her room.

After my morning shower, I went into one of the bathroom stalls. I stood with a pad in hand, looking at the toilet as if everything in the stall was unfamiliar. *Should I sit or stand?* I chose to stand. I dropped my underwear

143

halfway down my legs and placed the pad at the center, as Alinafe had instructed. I slid them back up. The pad formed two bulges near my crotch and backside. It was uncomfortable, like walking with a giant stick protruding through your legs from one end to the other.

All day, I walked with my legs slightly parted. I couldn't focus in class, nor could I pay attention to what people said to me. My mind was on the dry white cotton that was shifting around in my underwear. When I walked, I worried that people could see it sticking out behind me like a tail. When I sat down, it angled upward like an erect penis. I constantly readjusted myself on my seat, sometimes petting my lap to see if I could feel the protrusion. By the end of the day, I had had enough of the bulges in my underwear and my duck-waddling walk. At 3 PM, when classes were over, I went back to the bathroom stall and peeled the bloodless pad from my underwear. I wrapped it up in tissue paper, placed it in a plastic bag and threw it in the trash.

Walking around with a pad between my legs was a nightmare, but the twist was that it made me feel like a growing girl. I faked it for about four months. No one kept up with my lies. I had decided that on each monthly cycle, my period lasted for three days. Sometimes I asked friends for pads, other times I pretended I was wearing one. I barely checked my pad for potential overflow as Alinafe had suggested, or I did it for show—announcing, in a room full of girlfriends, that I was about to check it or that it was riding up my crotch again. Sometimes I spontaneously blurted out things like "Oh my God, my period is heavy this month," or "I need to lie down, I have terrible cramps."

Female pains, the struggles of being on the rag, were my way of showing off my femininity. I flaunted my growth through pretense. The more I did it, the more it felt real to me. Once, I was close to sharing my fake menstruation news with Kevin. "Hey, guess who's bleeding now?" I would whisper triumphantly in his ear. I didn't do it. Because a part of me feared his wise ways, his assessments of physical appearance, his peculiar wrist examinations.

People still teased me about having no breasts. Two girls targeted me in the showers after our weekly sports activities. I eventually started the habit of waiting for everyone to shower before I would take off my clothes. One day, I told my sports coach that I couldn't swim because I had my period and that I didn't wear tampons, but the truth was that I hated learning how to swim. There were three of us who were allowed to skip swimming, fearing we would bleed in the water. We sat on a bench by the pool, watching everyone get ready for the lessons. When Kevin and his friends passed, they snickered, asking us what was wrong and why we weren't swimming, when they obviously knew why. One girl told them to shut up. I was thrilled that Kevin would finally see me as a growing girl. I didn't respond to their questions, but I smiled, looking at the ground. I was one of the big girls, worthy of being wanted in every way by a boy. There was more snickering. Then heckling.

"*Choka iwe! Bala losapolalo!*" one of the boys shouted. Translation: "Get out of here, you, with your wound that never heals!"

My body always seemed to fall short and the teasing never stopped. My list of worries grew long: no breasts, flat backside, hairless legs, and now my vagina was an open wound that would never heal but bleed and repulse boys. That's when I realized pretending was pointless. Growing up was messy and disorienting. Being a girl confused me.

Running With Malaria

We ran laps from sideline to sideline on the netball court. The sun was hitting hard on our skin and sweat became visible on our foreheads, others had it rolling down their cheeks and shirts. On the school netball team at twelve years old, I was expected to do my best as the captain, to set an example for my teammates. But this afternoon, I felt chills that coursed through me as I stood on the field or as I ran. It was a hot, sunny day, yet my body could not warm up. My legs grew weak. If we stopped for a second on one sideline, I could feel my stance was wobbly, so I kept moving. I rubbed my biceps with my hands, hoping to create warmth. Nothing. Miss Bell blew a whistle to signal when to begin running after a stop on each line. About seven laps in, I stopped running. I was panting, and I walked towards her next to the sideline near trees that cast shade on the court.

"Miss Bell, I think I'm getting sick," I said, still panting—now shivering.

Miss Bell was a short white woman with an athletic body. She liked wearing shorts made out of wool and collared t-shirts. She was about 5'3, small dark eyes, short hair which reached her cheeks, parted at the center. Her legs were thin and strong-looking. Her wide smile was always encouraging and radiant. But on this day, she wasn't smiling at me. Miss Bell had become familiar with my ways of pretending or showing off during sporting activities. She knew I sought attention and each time she caught me doing it, she put a stop to narcissistic ways.

"Oh, come on!" she said with strong disbelief. "Finish running laps and you'll feel better," then she grinned with certainty that she had caught me faking again.

"I'm serious, Miss…I'm coming down with something," I pleaded.

She shook her head and continued blowing the whistle for each lap. I walked back to the line, still shivering, but hoping if I ignored the chills and weakness, maybe my mind would convince my body that I was not ill.

Whistle. I ran. Whistle. I ran.

The sun beamed on my skin but all I felt were body tremors that made me want to cry out for help as I grew weaker and weaker. My heart raced and a salty taste built up in my mouth. For a second, I thought Miss Bell was right, I doubted my own reasoning and emotions, but my denial of being ill was met with the pressure of my racing thoughts and failing body. Again, I stopped running.

"Miss, I need to get to the clinic. I'm not okay," I begged again.

"Just finish, Carol. Enough of this," she said dismissively and blew her whistle again.

By the time the netball exercises were over, my legs shook from the adrenaline and whatever else was happening to my body. Still dressed in my navy blue shorts and blue t-shirt, I walked across the school buildings and lawns to the clinic, which was located about a mile or more away from the sports field. I sat on a bench inside the hospital examination room as I watched the nurse prick my finger to draw blood for screening. I hated needles and the sting always made me jerk a little. I could never get used to it.

Malaria plus-three. I was diagnosed and immediately asked to go and lie down in one of the patient rooms. There are four levels of malaria depending on the severity. Plus-four is the worst. My temperature rose and fell throughout the day. I was in the clinic by myself. It was a rectangular room with four beds, two on either side of the room. I thought of the running I had endured that afternoon. *How on earth did I manage to run with malaria plus-three?* I wondered what Miss Bell would say since she had dismissed me as a liar when I was telling the truth. I hoped she would feel bad. Maybe guilty. It annoyed me when someone made a false accusation of me, especially if it was sports-related. Being great at sports had me labeled as a show-off. Although this was true at times, I wished people could see through me in moments when I was humble and sincere.

My goal was to avoid throwing up. This was the worst part of malaria. I sat up on my bed, wearing a white hospital gown with blue flowers. It was now evening and I had broken a sweat which drenched me, making my gown damp. The room was steadier than the swirling I experienced when I arrived. *How could a tiny mosquito bring down a human being like this?* I thought. So, I refrained from eating solid food for a while. Ginger ale was the best thing for settling my stomach. I drank plenty of water.

One day, the door flew open and in walked Miss Bell.

"So you weren't pretending after all," she said with a smile.

"You could have killed me," I said, grinning back at her.

I liked Miss Bell. She seemed like a quiet teacher, but when she spoke, her face lit up. She had taught me how to run the school road race without stopping very often. She taught me about a runner's longevity, and I always wanted to impress her with my stamina. We small-talked for a while, but I felt embarrassed to be seen in such a weak state. I even smiled at her when I was so close to collapse. I found myself constantly adjusting myself, pulling up the blanket to cover my body, wiping the sides of my mouth to avoid saliva from creating white foam, and fixing my hair. The clinic was a space where all your efforts to look good in public were completely thwarted. I had to settle for looking disheveled.

Malaria is a topsy-turvy illness. Aside from the hot and cold flashes, there is a ringing in the ears which interrupts your thought process. Food becomes tasteless, not to mention the frequent need to hurl out anything you eat. At home, my mother always took care of me. She gave me fresh cut tomatoes and onions. The sour tastes remove the need to feel sick, she said. At Kamuzu Academy, I did not have this care, but there was a nurse we called Aunt Sue, who brought home-cooked food—nsima, beef stew, and vegetables which I enjoyed after a few days of recovering with quinine medication.

At night, I feared to sleep alone and she always let me sleep in the nurses' ward so I wouldn't feel lonely or frightened. Part of my fear was from rumors I had heard about hauntings and a girl named Nadine who was supposedly possessed by the devil. This was never proven. Nadine was a chubby girl with light skin. She was very quiet and I never saw her erupt into demonic convulsions the way people had described her. Once, I was sitting in my ward and she slowly sauntered across the green lawn near my room. My heart raced when I saw her, but she looked like a deer in nature as if she was testing her surroundings of flowers, brown soil, rocks, and wild plants I could not name. But Nadine was the least of my worries. My malaria was really bad. My temperature was not going down, and my parents had to arrange that I return home in Blantyre. Since malaria has the potential to kill a person, my parents wanted to be the ones to take care of me.

There was a rumor about me on campus. Apparently, I had malaria plus-four instead of three. I only found out about the gossip after Mr. Mosten, our school pool attendant, had sold me mangoes. It fascinated me how people can stretch a story about someone's illness for dramatic purposes. At first, I chuckled at how severely people can embellish a story about why someone isn't around. Then, I realized that when my parents took me home to recover for a few days, people may have assumed that my sickness was very serious.

I recovered on quinine and healthy eating. My brother, Charles, even came to visit me when I was at the clinic. He wasn't the most affectionate brother, but he tried his best to be there for me. I remember when a dirty fan was placed in my room for cool air, he told Aunt Sue that he didn't want me inhaling filthy air. He looked so upset, very concerned. This was one of a few instances where I saw that he cared for me at school. Just because he didn't show his emotions often didn't mean he wasn't feeling them.

When I came out of the clinic, I realized that my sporty demeanor made people conclude that I was just showing off, preventing others from seeing me as someone who could be vulnerable. Miss Bell liked me, but her observation about me was mistaken because she thought I was stronger than I was and because she knew my teenage attitude all too well. I don't blame her for seeing me that way. It only shows how deceptive the symptoms of malaria can be.

I tried to speed up my recovery. Although I may have looked well some afternoons, I would still struggle with the shivers and chills that crept through my body when I least expected them. I was taking risks to feel better when only the process of recovery was what was really curing me. Slowly, my body healed—even when I didn't realize it. Finally, my mind could reason things again, and I could breathe again with ease. My days became brighter and brighter, and I decided I would never risk trying to recover too quickly again—because malaria only lingered and returned, if I tried to force things before I was really ready.

I got back to my normal school routine, but I became more conscientious about how I carried myself in class and during sports. My experience with malaria changed me. After that, I did everything I could to not ever suffer from it again. I avoided mosquitoes as much as I could. I know it is a bundle of bad fate that lies in the bite of a single mosquito. But moving to America would also remove any chance of ever being bitten by a malaria-infested mosquito again.

Malawian Girls Are Talented Too

I had a friend who thought America—all of America—belonged to white people. Agnes and I went to boarding school together at Kamuzu Academy. She was a tall, somewhat chubby, dark-skinned Malawian girl—very beautiful, but was often found with a "resting bitch face." You couldn't tell if she was mad, sad or depressed. Sometimes, she looked bored to death, as if she could fall asleep while sitting up. But when she smiled, her almond-shaped eyes would shine. She was very pretty. To Agnes, Blacks in America were an inferior species that only lived to work for white people, to make white lives better. It's not that Agnes wasn't a smart girl. In fact, she was of average intelligence. I say "average" mainly because she never asserted herself enough. Whether it was school work, hanging out with friends, doing her laundry or making ramen noodles, she had a certain passivity, a half-baked effort, even a laziness. I suspect that her views on America came from television, like many of us at Kamuzu Academy. However, her comprehension of reality versus fiction and of controversial issues on television was scrambled, making her a black Malawian girl who believed in white supremacist ideas of race.

I, on the other hand, had seen black African-American actors on T.V., but I was unsure if Africans who were not American could be cast in movies. On top of that, I didn't know any Malawian actresses, nor had I seen them performing until two years before I moved to America. I knew that some people saw Blacks as lesser than Whites because we had a very small community of white people in Malawi. At times, I sensed White fascination. Some black people idolized the difference in white people's features or how they spoke—perceptions that were highly influenced by Western-European aesthetics, the glorification of white skin, silky-blonde hair, blue eyes, green or gray. I liked white people fine and often got attracted to white boys, like the time when I was completely smitten by an actor named Jensen Ackles. Tall, brown hair, blues eyes, a perfectly symmetrical face, and a charming grin—he looked appetizing—my idea of a ten out of ten on the hotness rank. During vacation, I made sure I was home by 5 PM just in time to catch him on T.V. in a show called *Days of Our Lives*. I liked white people just fine, but never did I think America belonged to them.

My friends and I were seated in Agnes's room on a warm Saturday morning after our head mistress, Mrs. Banda, had inspected our rooms for cleanliness, the usual routine before attending assembly in the school auditorium. Most of the furniture was made of wood—a shimmering varnished golden-brown—two beds per room, both adjoined to desks on one end and lockers on the other. Mrs. Banda would slide her fingers on the edges of the furniture and then inspect the tips, tilting her head to look closely through her glasses.

"There should be no dust here," she would say with her part-Zimbabwean accent.

There was no excuse for missing a spot while cleaning. Mrs. Banda was a dust "po-po," skilled at excavating dirt like Sherlock Holmes zooming in on evidence with a magnifying glass. Our beds had to be neatly made, windows shined, clothes folded in drawers. Our uniforms were properly fitted and had to be worn well too. Gray mini-skirts were prohibited, no rolled-up shirt sleeves, green ties could not be worn loosely and socks had to be pulled up just below our knees (Never to be rolled down in public). Sock-bunching also had to be avoided. The Academy even provided garters to hold them up. Shoes had to be black. No matter where we were, if we failed to meet these requirements and Mrs. Banda noticed it, she would walk up to us and fix our uniforms—as if we were big babies who couldn't dress ourselves properly. She made sure she did it in front of people too.

In Agnes's room, some girls laid on the beds and others sat by the desks. The room inspection was over. We loosened our ties, rolled up our shirt sleeves and pushed down our socks. I sat at the corner of Agnes's bed. She sat on a chair by her desk. I don't remember how the topic came up, but we were discussing our dream jobs. As always, my friends wanted to be doctors, lawyers, and scientists. They mentioned their reasons—more money, saving innocent people, a love for mixing chemicals, following the footsteps of family members who had become said occupations. They all seemed so sure of their chosen careers. I was silent. But it was a time when I was also slowly gathering the courage to voice out what I was passionate about.

"Me, I don't know," Agnes said, looking outside the window as if she was done with the conversation.

I jumped up from the bed and made a silly pose, extending my arms, fingers spread out, knees slightly bent, like I was presenting something to a crowd. Then, I popped my eyes wide open and gave a cheesy grin. Think Jim Carrey in the movie *Ace Ventura: Pet Detective* or *The Mask*.

"Guess what *I'm* going to be?!" I shouted at the center of the room.

Everyone laughed.

"Eh, *koma* Carol you are trouble," Tadala said, shaking her head in mid-laughter. She was a very smart girl who always scored A's in almost every quiz, undeniably one of the top ten smartest girls in our cohort. She always laughed at my jokes, was ever captivated when I pretended to be different characters and when I sang songs or danced to music just for fun. Not everyone liked my shtick. To some, I was just an annoying friend. They simply rolled their eyes and walked away from me.

"An actress!" Fatsani shouted, joining me with a leap at the center. She enjoyed my quirkiness because *she* was quirky too. We goofed around together, often performing in dances we had choreographed ourselves for the yearly school variety show.

Agnes did not buy any of my acts. And I had grown accustomed to how my efforts to entertain friends were met with her resting bitch face. I never took offense. It was just the way she was. At least that's what I told myself.

"You'll see me on T.V. in America one day!" I shouted, "While you dissect bodies and talk to Judges!" I jested some more, performing popular movie scenes, just to show them who I would be on screen, changing my accent whenever I wanted, striking my "Oh, *hell* no!" American poses. My body felt free when I pretended to be someone else. It loosened up. I stretched my limbs. Contorted— meticulously capturing the demeanor of different characters. If I had tension in my body, it seemed to vanish. My mind began to work fast, probably because of comedic timing. I made eye contact with my friends, engaged them with my characters, trying to create the biggest impact with my acting choices. The room boomed with laughter. After a few minutes, I felt the sweat on my forehead. I simmered down. It was almost time for assembly. Everyone grew silent. "*Inu,* we have to go," Tadala announced. Ties were tightened, socks were pulled up just below the knees, shirt-sleeves rolled out. Agnes snickered, looking at my sweaty face.

"What?" I said. Laughing with her. A part of me was happy that she was finally entertained by my act.

Agnes shook her head. "Let's be serious now," she said, "You can't do this in America. No one will want you there. America is for white people. You're black!"

I froze. My smile faded. I had no defense against her words. My friends were already walking out of the room, no one had paid attention to Agnes's remark, so no one defended me. There would be no running to mother for consolation either. She was in another city, six hours away. I gave no reply, straightened out my uniform and walked out of Agnes's room, humiliated—for having black skin. I wondered if this, too, was why my father did not want me to become an actress. Was he hiding his thoughts about my skin on purpose? Was he protecting me from embarrassment for being black? I didn't know what to think. But I ached. Instead of walking towards the auditorium for assembly, I ran to my bedroom. I slammed the door, threw myself on my bed, curled up and cried to God—asking him why he did that to me, why he made me black.

*

Love Triangles. Double-lives. Relationships corrupted by witchcraft. These were popular themes for our school plays. At Kamuzu Academy, we were encouraged to be creative story-tellers as well as performers. My friends and I would huddle up in one room and throw storylines at each other to bring our characters to life. Our school was very much like Harry Potter's Hogwarts, just without the magic. We were divided into houses like Gryffindor and Slytherin, but boys and girls were separated. The male houses were Chilanga, Chilowa and Mbelwa and the females had Kapeni, Gomani, and Mlonyeni. I was in Kapeni. So if we wrote plays, the girls had to perform male roles as well. We had a huge fascination with love and attraction, probably because we were also figuring out our own experiences with intimacy. In our stories, we explored courtship, seduction, how to build strong and faithful relationships, and we shunned cheating. Our characters not only struggled with love and finding true happiness, but something in their lives would always make it difficult to provide for their families.

Either they had difficulty finding a job or they would get fired from one. Money issues led to arguments within the family, chances of cheating would rise and if a character was really down and desperate, they would consult a witchdoctor for a magical boost with fate—something we had learned that people experienced in real life.

At first, I was cast in minor roles. Auditioning was not my strongest suit. Part of the problem was how my body made me feel. I was very small and skinny, but I was used to playing vigorous activities with boys, climbing trees, war games, and crazy bicycle stunts. I moved in paths that were associated with masculinity, unafraid to make big, grand, daring gestures. My posture was also very athletic. One term, when I was eleven years old, I was on stage in the school auditorium, about to audition in front of a panel of five senior class students who were directing a play they had written. I walked into the auditorium in blue baggy jeans and a white t-shirt with a zebra on the front. I looked like a little boy, which I tried to cover up by letting my braids loose. When they gave me a script to read the part of a girl who was having relationship problems with her boyfriend, I did not know how to make myself vulnerable. There was a feminine fragility that came with a soft voice and a delicate body frame. As I performed the scene with another girl who played the character's boyfriend, my body became tighter and tighter. Before I could begin to understand what the lines meant, I found I had difficulty even moving like a girl. I tried to affect a more casual posture—dropping my shoulders a little to make myself look less stiff. I then arched my back more, since backsides were an attractive quality on girls, but mine, at that age, was flat. Yet, standing with a curved spine only made me look as if I was desperate to use the bathroom. And when I moved across the stage, you would think I was learning how to walk. I was better off standing in one spot, which only made my audition boring.

There was no motive. My line delivery had no vocal inflection, no purpose, and my character wasn't fighting for anything. My body had failed me. After I finished the scene, I dreaded looking at the panel. And when I lifted my eyes from the script, I saw what I feared—sympathetic faces that looked like they were hiding a secret from me, as if a terrible misfortune had occurred and they didn't want me to find out that I had caused it. I had known my audition was a disaster, seconds into the start of my performance. Nasmeen, a mixed-race girl who was one of the directors, stood up from the panel.

"Okay, *good*!" she said, with an unconvincing smile. She gathered some papers.

"Here. Try playing this kid," she said, holding out the script. I walked over and grabbed it. "This kid wakes up in the middle of the night and she is wondering where her father is. Just try it." She sat back down.

I nodded, scared to screw up again. The directions were to walk into the living room with my teddy bear and tell my mother I could not sleep, then proceed to ask where my father was. I walked to the left-wing of the stage and took a deep breath. Since I was playing a child, I didn't worry about my body frame. I was already small in size and it was working to my advantage. All I had to worry about was looking cute, adorable. Who didn't want to look good on stage? I wrapped my arms around the side of my waist, pretending to hold a teddy bear. Then, I entered the stage, rubbing my eyes to show that I had been sleeping.

"Mommy, I can't sleep," I whined with a sleepy voice. Then I exchanged a few more words with the girl playing my mother. She seemed like a natural. She was taller than me, had a bigger body frame with all the curves in the right places and a nurturing demeanor with her affectionate embrace—motherly indeed. We sat on two metal chairs, which were meant to represent a couch at center stage, as she explained that my father (who was probably somewhere cheating or consulting a witchdoctor) would be home soon and that I needed to go back to bed. Pretending to be a child was easier, way easier than putting on a feminine posture. There was no need to modify my body in ways I was not used to. Instead, I performed with ease. The panel loved it. They clapped and gave me a standing ovation at the end. I had redeemed myself from my previous acting misfortune.

*

I nailed it—every time I performed male roles, for obvious reasons. As a male character, I could move freely. It was a body freedom similar to how I felt when I played with boys or when I played sports. My favorite part was not having to wear heels. To me, heels were torture devices for women. As a male, I walked on stage with a swagger of command, extending myself, making big gestures, expressing my body language in larger ways than what was expected of females in Malawi—on or off stage. I wore loose, comfortable costumes, suits, baggy jeans, over-sized t-shirts (since most boys copied the looks of male hip-hop rappers) and I even liked wearing ties. This was something I had associated strongly with the meticulous businessman-look that my father often had, and how he approved of my brothers' fashion if they wore a suit and tie.

"Yes, this is how you dress up," he would say to my brothers, "Not these over-sized shirts with numbers on the back like American rappers."

A part of me knew I could never impress my father dressed in a suit and tie because such clothes were not meant for girls. Malawians wouldn't know what to do with me. However, another part of me enjoyed the fiction I lived on stage, in male attire, because I had subconsciously internalized my father's fashion ideals. I knew other tomboys like me on campus, but we never talked about any desire to dress up like a boy. Most girls who put on oversized t-shirts either thought of it as a cool look or they flaunted clothing they borrowed from their boyfriends. Wearing your boyfriend's shirt announced the person you were dating. People paid attention to fashion, and they could recognize which clothes belonged to whom.

I had to flirt as a man on stage. It would be my last performance at Kamuzu Academy. I was fifteen years old and I was playing a man who was having an affair. The woman's role was performed by my roommate, Mia. For a costume, she wore blue jean capris and a turquoise tank top. I wore a white long-sleeved collared shirt, loose black suit-pants, and a black belt to hold them up. The suit jacket was in my right hand, hanging on my shoulder. I remember walking from stage left to meet Mia's character at the bottom of the wooden brown stairs that were connected to the stage at the center. Mia sat at the edge of the third step, her light brown skin glowed from the stage lights. Her shoulders were slightly hunched, reducing the size of her body, hands held together at the center of her belly. She looked protective of herself, even with the faint smile she had on stage. Her body looked as if it could collapse at any moment, or as if the wind could easily blow her off the stairs. She looked fragile and uncomfortable. Yet, *there* was the familiar feminine form I lacked. The missing posture that rendered me alien—an anomaly, an imposter of the female gender. I walked towards Mia with my swagger of command, loving the spotlight. Part of me wishing I could carry myself like Mia to fit in with other girls, and another part feeling relieved that playing a male role was freeing me from an uncomfortable demeanor. Even better, having no worries about my body would allow me to give my best performance and to deliver my lines with purpose and intention. I could unleash a powerful stage presence that could make people feel things, and I could move an audience just like my mother did with the President Kamuzu Banda. But most of all, I could become a fictional male character who felt more real and truer to my physical nature than the female life I lived off stage.

*

Hurt from my father's disapproval of acting and friends like Agnes who made me feel insecure about being a black actress, I blocked and ignored. Months before I moved to America, I colored my imagination with fantasies of acting beside the handsome Michael Ealy, Denzel Washington, and Jensen Ackles, as a sidekick detective or superhero. No surprise that my mind started gravitating towards roles that complemented my athletic, tomboy personality. I wanted clever roles with fast line-pickups, impeccable comedic timing, and maybe a little sass. I imagined myself on set in America, cameras all around me. Some zooming in for a close-up shot of my face as I performed complex emotions. Others capturing my body, which would bloom into my mother's Foxy Cleopatra shape during her acting days. Mine would be a Coca-Cola bottle-shaped body with a short pixie haircut like Halle Berry because America would accept that short hair looked good on women, too. My mother would watch T.V. with my father in the living room. She would gasp with excitement at the sight of me on screen, then point at my performance: "Look-look-look!" she would say to my father, proud that I am finally fulfilling the acting dream she lost as a child. Hollywood would bring out my glamor, showcasing my intelligence and wit. The world would see that I, a Malawian girl, was talented and beautiful too. Something that I think would have made President Kamuzu Banda proud.

Try Again

A plane had crashed shortly after takeoff, about 200 feet from the runway. Eight passengers. Zero survivors. On T.V. was a white aircraft, a twin-engine Cessna 402B, completely destroyed. All that was left was the mid-section of the plane. Everything else, rubble. At the bottom of the screen was a headline: *Pop Star Aaliyah Dead in Plane Crash.* I was on my parents' bed, laying on my belly with my legs crossed in the air. When I saw the headline, I jumped up on the bed. "No!" I shouted, holding my head. It was August of 2001, and I was fourteen years old. I reached for the remote and turned up the volume. My mind flashed with images of Aaliyah dancing in her music videos, *Try Again*, *Are You That Somebody*. Her black bandana wrapped around her head, her black long hair flowing perfectly beside her cheeks, her smooth hip-hop dance slides to the sides, front and back—ever so effortless. There was nobody on the T.V. screen, just a camera panning around the shattered plane. My memory of the news is in broken words. She had boarded a plane in the Bahamas around 6:50 PM. She had just finished filming the music video for her song, *Rock the Boat*. Filming finished earlier than anticipated. Aaliyah and friends were eager to return to

America. They were warned not to board the plane because it was overloaded with luggage. They boarded it anyway. It crashed. She was 22 years old.

I cried as though Aaliyah and I had been childhood friends. She was my favorite female hip-hop artist, at the top of my list of concerts to attend if I moved to America. I wanted to carry myself the way she did on T.V.; there was a calm and collected air about her, but nothing close to a passive demeanor. Aaliyah shared the different sides of her female identity. On her 1994 album CD cover, *Age Ain't Nothing but a Number*, Aaliyah wore all black, dark sunglasses, a t-shirt and a jacket with a hood on her head. She looked like a tough fourteen-year-old girl. Gangster. On her 1996 album CD cover, *One in a Million*, she wore a black jacket, a red blouse slightly exposed and dark sunglasses—a mysterious sixteen-year-old girl. Fierce, and more feminine than her previous CD cover. For her 2001 album cover, *Aaliyah*, she wore a light, brown sleeveless V-neck blouse, her arms in the sides with her back arched, highlighting her broad shoulders. Long black curly hair flowed down her back, which was set against a red background. Her head tilted to the side—smoky dark eyes—and her mouth slightly opened as if she were in the middle of singing something. This was a very feminine twenty-two-year-old Aaliyah. Sexy. Her smile was contagious. And when she grinned on screen, I grinned too, even if I didn't know what she was grinning about. There was diversity in her looks, and if Aaliyah could be more than one kind of girl, then I wanted my identity to be as fluid as hers.

Aaliyah was a girl who wasn't afraid to dance half-naked on T.V. In the late 90s, a Malawian girl would be shamed if she ever attempted it, whether on T.V. or not. In Aaliyah's music videos, she either showed her belly wearing a blouse that looked more like a bra, or she wore leather pants with tight tops. She made girls with slim, slender bodies like mine look good. The best part was that you didn't need to have a big backside to be considered attractive. Her outfits also portrayed her tomboy personality, a mixture of masculinity with her baggy jeans, femininity with her tight blouses, and an edge with her bandanas. Her attire made me embrace the shape of my body because there was balance in her dress code—a harmony, providing my tomboy personality with a solution for the discomfort I felt when my body was in feminine clothes.

*

We watched Aaliyah's music videos over and over again, my high school friends and I, whenever we were on vacation. Our goal was to mimic every dance move in the videos for *Try Again* and *We Need a Resolution*. We had to perform the dances at our school variety show. So we watched how fluidly Aaliyah's body moved to the tempo and rhythm of the music, then attempted to reenact that same smoothness with which she moved. We wrote the dance steps in our notebooks. Then, when we returned to school, Mia, Fatsani, Chimwemwe, and I practiced in one of our dorm rooms. We tied our t-shirts into knots at our backs, revealing our bellies, just like Aaliyah did in the video for *Are You That Somebody*. To better capture what Aaliyah looked like when she moved, we chose to practice in baggy or tight pants. Chimwemwe, a short girl with big bedroom eyes and a kind smile, was the one who had first memorized Aaliyah's moves from *Try Again*. She was also the most flexible. Always patient at teaching us Aaliyah's styles. She helped us with precision, showing us how far to stretch our arms, which way to cross our legs, or how to sway our necks from side to side. She would watch us do dance combinations, over and over again, until we moved in unison. There were also sections of the music that required our own creativity. When one of us pressed play on our blue and silver boombox radio, everyone found a space in the room to explore the music. We taught ourselves how to listen, interpret and dance to songs. We set the rhythm of our dance to the sound, used an 8-count to determine when to do each move, our minds interpreted musicality, while our bodies expressed movements that illustrated anything we felt in the music. If someone came up with a dance move we all liked, we kept it in the main choreography of the song.

Unlike my struggle with imitating a feminine posture in acting, my slim body was perfect for dancing. I swayed, slid, bent, dropped and jumped with no worry about whether I looked girly enough or not. All I had to work on was my flexibility. I sharpened my precision with hip-hop moves— a mixture of hard and soft gestures, which, to me, felt like another harmony between masculinity and femininity. If we failed to bend, twist, curl or arch ourselves the way Aaliyah did, we would "try again," stopping and starting the music if we needed to be sharper, if we needed to synchronize our steps better. We practiced for hours and hours until our bodies loosened up. Each time we failed to get it right, we were eager to try again.

There was also liberation in how Aaliyah allowed her body to bend and twist in big and small ways. She was precise with her smooth slides, head-shakes, chest-pops, and arm and leg work. You would think she had no bones. Even better, she moved like a female version of another one of my favorite dance artists, Michael Jackson. Of course, Aaliyah's dancing had a hip-hop twist to it, but to see a female Michael Jackson was groundbreaking for me. Her body flowed to music in ways that made me want to express myself through movement, just like I did with acting. I had found a female icon I could imitate, someone that made me feel comfortable in my own skin. If my body was ever stiff and unappealing with its lack of curves, I had found a new language in dancing. This was a language that wasn't dependent on big breasts, backsides and wide hips but a language that encouraged me to let my body be as it is. I moved in ways that didn't alienate me from my body but, instead, helped me understand it by discovering what I could become as I flowed to the music. It is magical how people who do not know each other, people who live in different parts of the world, can become connected through art. Aaliyah's music had created a bond between us. It made me feel close to her. Even closer to American culture. We enjoyed being different kinds of girls, Aaliyah and I. And losing her was losing a part of myself—my childhood friend.

The Devil's Playground

Our green Kamuzu Academy school bus pulled up at the front of Mount Soche Hotel in Blantyre City on a hot Friday afternoon and my teammates and I cheered at our arrival. Our coaches shushed us. We were at a High School sports meet for netball and soccer and since we were in boarding school, we had travelled six hours from Kasungu for a meet that was scheduled for Sunday. Most of us were from Blantyre, so the school required that we stay in our homes, but my fifteen-year-old friends and I had other plans.

"We're not allowed to stay at home," I lied to my father on the phone.

"But why? You have always come home during school trips," he said, puzzled.

"*Kaya*, but the school already organized a place for us to sleep…maybe they don't want us wandering off with our own agendas."

"Oh…is that so?" he said with a serious tone. "Where?"

I could sense the skepticism, sarcasm even. "I think Mount Soche Hotel?"

My friends, who stood around me to listen, jerked my body with their hands, mouthing the word "cottage," reminding me of the specifics of our lie.

"Well, some are staying at Mount Soche and others at a cottage in Namiwawa. I'll let you know where I end up," I said, knowing exactly where I would end up.

"Okay…" Brief silence. "But Ms. Kautsire…*be careful*," he said.

His caution gave me the chills, as if he already knew I was up to no good. I gave a thumbs up to my friends who would do the same with their parents. One by one, we lied. The plan was for six of us to stay at Tiya's parents' cottage in Namiwawa, twenty minutes away from my house in Sunny Side. We would have the cottage to ourselves for the whole weekend, with a house servant to cook and clean for us. We had until Sunday to party as hard as we could—no parents, no teachers, no curfews.

The drinking began the moment we arrived at the cottage—a three-bedroom, cream-colored brick house with brown wooden doors, gray cement pathways, and green hedges and shrubs surrounding the yard. We laid around on sofas in the living room, drinking Malawi Gin and Premier Brandy with coke and sprite, plotting how to maneuver the night.

"We need rides, *magaye,*" Martha said, sipping on her drink.

"Then let's make some calls," Tiya said, standing up. "We'll need to hit up some guys, so go through your phones." She made a loud clap with her hands, like two cymbals—a gesture that was popular at Kamuzu Academy. We associated it with our math teacher, Mrs. La Rouche, who would clap her hands really loud whenever she was thrilled or outraged about something. Then, she would stretch the pronunciation of words, as if she were about to break into a slow song. Her unique emotional reactions made students laugh, and many of us adopted her mannerisms. The clapping was one of many. We scrolled through our phones, each of us shouting the names of boys with cars—friends, cousins, past boyfriends, never-ending flings, friends who knew friends with cars. I didn't know many boys with cars and either my former boyfriends didn't have one, or the men I knew with rides were friends of my brothers—territory I didn't want to mess with. In the middle of drinking and making calls, I thought of how I missed my parents. I hadn't seen them for weeks after going to boarding school. This trip was an opportunity to see them, but I was choosing not to, preferring the freedom to party without worrying about restrictions. I watched my friends in action: flashing screens in their faces, smiling, talking with soft voices, giggling, flicking their braids. I wondered if any of them secretly missed their parents too, if they were hiding fear beneath their smiles. But this was a weekend we would go against our parents, we would break their rules and expectations: "Work hard in school," "Don't let boys distract you," "A girl must cook and clean at home," and "No sex, drugs, and alcohol." We would indulge in debauchery instead.

"I hope we don't bump into our parents," I said. Joking, but nervous.

Everybody laughed. Some stood up and did the clapping gesture.

"Scandal!" We all shouted.

I gulped down my gin and sprite, hoping for a buzz. I knew I needed liquid courage.

Friday nights were on fire at a club called Legends. It was right at the heart of Blantyre City, ten minutes away from our cottage. The chances of getting rides from guys were high since it wasn't far. We took turns showering, then tried on different club outfits. Tight jeans, boob tubes, blouses that showed lots of skin—something our parents wouldn't allow us to walk out in. We covered ourselves with jean jackets, a temporary part of our attire to fend off the cool evening breeze. The jackets would fly off our bodies when the dancing got intense. We let loose our braids and our flat-ironed chemically relaxed hair. Some put on make-up. I knew nothing about make-up. Some practiced their walking in heels. I stayed away from heels (because watching me in heels was like watching a newborn baby goat try to walk). Tiya had called a friend to pick us up; he also lived in Namiwawa. At around 10 PM, when a black four-wheel-drive pulled into the yard, six fifteen-year-old girls packed themselves inside of it.

"Hello ladies!" the man said.

A drunken chorus of hellos sounded from the backseat of the car.

As we drove through Blantyre City, I smiled at the thought of being home. But something was off. Even though things looked familiar, I felt like I was on vacation in some other land. Then, it occurred to me that home didn't feel like home because I wasn't staying with my parents. When we got to the club, the music was pumping. Men and boys walked around with Carlsberg beer bottles, some dressed in baggy clothes, headbands, caps tilted to the side; others were still in business attire, suits and ties even. Women paraded in tight clothes, short dresses, and mini-skirts, cleavage everywhere. If parents witnessed their children in this Dionysian scene, they would doubt all their parenting methods. When we got out of the car, I recognized the man who was driving us—a dark-skinned man with a goatee and sideburns, a charming smile. I could see him from the rare view mirror. He was friends with my brother, Trevor. I started hiding my face. It amazed me that I had ridden in the backseat of his car and he had no clue who was with him. If we got into a car accident, who would he say was in his car? But at the time, I was only relieved that the darkness of the backseat was concealing my identity. If anyone as much as resembled someone my brothers or parents knew, I would hide my face.

We drank Smirnoff Ice after Smirnoff Ice, gin and tonic after gin and tonic. It was like a race to make up for all the alcohol we were warned not to drink. Hip-hop music filled the room. We made a circle on the dance floor and took turns dancing at the center, mixing both rigid and fluid hip-hop dance moves with African butt-shaking dance. Men attempted to break into the circle, but our rule was simple: if we found them cute, we gave them access. If not, we synchronized our dance moves, slowly moving the circle away from anyone undesirable. Some men used other methods to dance with us. They would dance next to you and take you by the arm, gently pulling you toward them, hoping you will give into the swaying of their bodies. Age didn't seem to matter either. One second, a young guy in his teens or 20s would try to grind up on you and next, a man old enough to be your father was pulling your arm towards him with a come-hither grin. I imagined a drunken man knowing my father, tugging at my arm as he slowly recognized the resemblance.

"Aren't you Ben Kautsire's daughter?" he would say, wagging a finger at me, trying his best to steady himself.

It was what most parents called "the devil's playground," and my teenage friends and I were now in the middle of the field. Sloppy kissing. Hands sliding up skirts. Glowing marijuana blunts and smoke everywhere. People passed out in corners of the club, some throwing up. There was dancing that looked like dry-humping and gyration that looked like it could knock someone up. This was the life that our church-going parents didn't want us to be a part of. This playground, we were told, was where people fell into sin, especially young girls who didn't yet know enough about life. I was very familiar with the process of sinful manifestation and how it resulted in a life of damnation: first, the young girl indulges in alcohol and drugs (willingly or through peer pressure), her sound mind and judgment fly out the window, which makes her end up in bed with men she doesn't know. Next, the horrors are unleashed— unprotected sex, broken condoms, rape. Or things could get darker: unwanted pregnancy, contraction of diseases, abortion, murder—her innocence, forever lost to sexual misfortunes. Knowing this process was enough to limit my curiosity about sex and drugs.

First of all, I feared marijuana. Smoking it was taboo during my teens. In Malawi, if you smoked pot, you were equivalent to a mad person who roams around the streets in smelly clothes, talking gibberish. I stayed away from it, didn't even touch cigarettes. Secondly, I feared sex so much that I began to mentally condemn friends who told me about their sexual experiences, even if they were positive. They were Hester Prynnes. Shame on them for having any kind of sex, and actually enjoying it. One friend, Pilirani, tried to explain how she had had sex in a bathroom stall at a lounge where we often played pool and drank gin and tonics all day, our favorite pastime. The bathroom was a tiny rectangular space that only fit a toilet and a sink on the side of the wall. If you stood up from the toilet seat, you could take four steps forward and reach the entrance.

"He sat on the toilet, I climbed on top of him, and we just started going at it," Pilirani said, exhaling menthol cigarette smoke from her nose.

"Oh, wow…weren't you afraid of breaking the condom?" A question I often asked when she explained anything about sex.

"Nah," she said. "Why worry about that stuff when the point is to feel good?"

I, on the other hand, couldn't imagine getting out of my head during sex. Each hump would potentially break the condom, and if it broke, who knew what diseases I would be contracting. What if I thought I had protected sex and a month later, I started throwing up because there was a hole in the condom? I imagined my mother's sad face, how she might feel she had failed at raising me. My father's rage, his disappointment. What if he kicked me out of the house? I knew there was abortion, but I had also heard that people could die from it. My fear of sex grew enormously.

Our Friday night at Legends was a victory at living our lie, how partying mattered more than seeing our parents. There were no mishaps. No one had sex with a man they did not know. No one got into a fight. No one got sick. Only close friends recognized us, and we all got home safe. We were the lucky ones, the ones who survived what parents feared. But there was also Saturday, a night with a different story. This night would show us how the devil could switch strategies at any time, on *his* playground.

*

Hangovers were our only consequence of Friday night's partying. We spent all morning sleeping them off. When we finally woke up to a sunny Saturday afternoon, the smell of rice and chicken stew reached our bedrooms. The lunch was ready. We dragged our exhausted bodies to the dining room and made our plates, proceeding to drink more alcohol. Drinking time was anytime from noon onwards. I always wondered who came up with this rule. Did people really need to justify when it was okay to drink? Or did it have something to do with reducing the guilt of drinking at hours where one needed to be sober and responsible for life? Not that one can't be responsible while drinking. We were back on gin and brandy. It was nice to have food in our stomachs again, nice to not have to cook and clean up after ourselves. We watched Austin Powers, all of us captivated by his openness toward sex. Tiya and I were even obsessed with the name of Austin's car—Shaguar.

"Fine! We'll both claim it as a nickname!" Tiya shouted, doing the famous hand clap, "But we'll see who gets it to stick. The one who gets known for it wins."

For months, I wrote "Shaguar" on my school books, artwork, sports t-shirts. People referred to me by it and I even used it for my email address (an address I would later regret for professional reasons). It was clear I had won the nickname. I don't think Tiya was as serious as I was. It was just part of a childish fascination with a quirky British man who was very enthusiastic about sex, ever so horny. Sex was naughty. And naughty is what we wanted to be.

Two cars—three girls in each one. That's the best we could find for Saturday night. The men driving, mid-to-late twenties, were strangers to me. I didn't know if they were responsible drivers, sober or drunk. But this was less of a concern because I was too busy being excited that we got a ride in the first place. Soul City was the name of the club. It was located on Zomba Road in Blantyre City, an area that did not have a lot of street lights. It was more of a dark forest. In other words, Soul City was a club in the middle of nowhere.

It was beautiful on the inside. Disco globes spun colors around, the walls were mirrors that reflected everyone dancing, the beat of hip-hop music shot through our feet the moment we stepped on the dance floor. We formed our usual circle, sticking together was important at packed nightclubs. We kept track of each other. On this night, we scanned the room for cute guys. *We* were the seekers. After surviving one night of advances from boys and men, we were now brave veterans, using our bodies to inch in on those whom we found attractive, hoping they would turn their bodies towards us, hoping they would hold us and move with us. I had many successes. Only a few epic fails— especially the ones whose angry girlfriends would suddenly appear and yank them away, leaving me with a vicious stare. This went on until early morning, around 1 AM. A few of us felt tired and it seemed like a good time to head home. Besides, we had a netball game to play on that same day, not to mention a six-hour drive back to Kamuzu Academy after the meet.

The men who drove us to the club were nowhere to be found. At one point, I stood at the entrance of the club, looking for faces I didn't even know. All I saw were staggering unfamiliar men and women. The search felt pointless. The next thing I knew, someone had a friend with a pickup truck that was heading toward our cottage in Namiwawa. Out of exhaustion, and desperation, the girls and I felt it was better to get closer to our cottage than to be stuck standing outside a nightclub in the middle of nowhere. Three of us got into the truck. Tiya and the other two were brave enough to stay behind and find another ride. I didn't know which group of three was wiser at the time. I stood next to Martha at the back of the truck holding onto the railing of the front hood. Drunk men were singing; others spewed profanities. Some sat in the sides of the truck, curled up from exhaustion; others still had beer bottles in their hands—a sight that would scare the Christ out of my parents. Now, I cringed at the thought of driving through a dark forest in the open air with a potentially drunk driver.

It happened halfway down a long dark road surrounded by tall blue-gum trees. At first, I thought the driver was too drunk to keep his foot on the gas pedal. The car began to slow down, a few sudden jerks, then loud noises emerged from the car exhaust. A huge commotion rose in the back, men complaining, banging the sides of the truck.

"Ahhhh! Drive properly, you idiot!" Someone shouted.

Then, we came to a complete stop. People lowered their voices, that moment when you realize the driver is not the problem. My heart raced.

"The car is out of gas!" The driver shouted outside his window.

This was not exactly the devil's playground, but it was one of his layers which my friends and I had fallen into. It was pitch black. The only lights on were car headlights. We stood amongst men we did not know. I thought of where I was in the process of sinful manifestation: alcohol—check, lack of sound judgment—check, and although I wasn't having sex, I had put myself in a situation where rape and murder could have occurred through men I did not know. This was Saturday's lesson, my consequence for lying to my father, for chasing debauchery while shunning my parents' caution.

I prayed, in my heart, hoping no one would touch us, that nothing would leap out of the bushes to harm us. A few cars passed by but none stopped to help. Martha used her cellphone to call Tiya. She was in a car heading home with the others, she would pass the street we were on. After minutes that felt like a lifetime of sitting in fear, a set of headlights slowed down behind our pickup. Tiya stuck her head out and called for us. We jumped out of the truck and ran towards the car. Men yelled profanities at us. Why? I will never know. We hadn't even spoken to them. Maybe it was the alcohol talking and since they were still stuck in the middle of a dark road, maybe all they could do was take out their frustration on us—the ones with a rescue ride. Some said we were "stupid bitches," others called us *mahule*, whores. And during a very silent, long ride back to our cottage, that was exactly how I felt, like a stupid bitch, a whore—a devil's play toy.

Not Going Back

I was fifteen when I completed high school at Kamuzu Academy. Because the school followed a British educational system that was subject-based, they offered over fifteen courses that led to the International General Certification of Secondary Education Examinations of the University of Cambridge. The first five years of high school were known as O-levels. At this stage, students studied all fifteen-plus courses. If a student added two more years to study a specific major, they were known as A-levels. Students who were drawn to sciences were the ones who were likely to do their A-levels. The sciences were held with high regard, and choosing the A-level path was a sign that a student was serious about education. It suggested a potential for academic excellence since the student would spend more time mastering their major. This student wasn't me. I did not choose two more years of high school.

The sciences didn't appeal to me. Sometimes I was partial to biology—the human body fascinated me—but I didn't care for other aspects of the subject enough to study it closely. I loved English literature but my writing was a disaster. Each year, my writing skills were below average. Other A-level courses such as Mathematics, Economics, and Accounting, didn't stick either. I hated dealing with numbers. Latin and Greek were an exception, but no one informed me about making a career out of classical studies. I worried that my father would think it was a joke, like acting. I nixed the thought of pursuing the classics. The only thing I was brilliant at was sports. Our deputy headmaster, Peter Howard, always suggested that I stick with sports as a career. With all the sports awards I was winning, he believed I had what it took to be a professional runner. True, I loved running, but I couldn't see it as a career. Besides, it wasn't offered for A-level studies.

During my last year at Kamuzu Academy, I had spoken to my brothers several times about schools in America. They had both moved to Boston, and I intended to follow their path. My mother was aware of how hard it was to get my father to understand my frustrations with education, so she encouraged me to ask my brothers for advice, for any alternatives that would appeal to my father. I envied my brothers for living in Boston. They were free to make their own professional choices, and I often begged to live with them. We knew that the only way to convince my father to send me abroad was through education. It was one of the most important things he cared about when it came to raising his children. My brothers began to sense my desperation when we spoke on the phone. I brought up the topic of school in every conversation. My mother often listened on the side.

"I don't like A-level subjects. Everything is so tough," I complained.

"Then why don't you ask Dad to start college here?" Trevor asked.

"What?"

"You don't have to do your A-levels if you don't want to. It'll be a waste of money."

"That's what I told Dad, but he won't listen," I whined.

"Tell him you can start college here. All you need are your O-level certificates."

This was true. With my IGCSE from Cambridge, I was eligible to begin college anywhere. I thought of my age. Some of my friends had told me that it was a mistake that I started high school at age nine, that my mind wasn't mature enough to grasp tough concepts. They said it was why I sometimes struggled with English grammar and math equations, no matter how thoroughly I studied for tests. I didn't know if this was true, but back then, I believed it. I became paranoid about it. And now, I worried that being fifteen would be a problem too.

"But Trevor, won't they think I'm too young for college in America?" I asked.

"You're not too young, *Iwe*," he insisted, "College is very easy here. You'll ace everything."

Trevor's reassurance was all it took to begin my campaign for college in America. Every day of my last year in high school, I fantasized about life in America. Everything would be easy. I imagined taking acting classes, teachers writing A's on my quizzes, putting my hand up in class to answer every question, teachers nodding at my profound contributions to class discussions, running track, playing soccer and basketball (I'd be captain of many sports teams in America too), and lots of friends would surround me. So I started spreading rumors about myself at school. Here were the facts: I was leaving Kamuzu Academy after my O-levels. I was moving to America to study acting. And I was never coming back to Malawi.

During holidays, I worked on convincing my father to send me abroad. I had a begging routine. Once, I knocked on my father's bedroom door. "Come in!" I walked in with my shoulders hunched, sulking, my eyes close to tears. I sat on his bed while he sat on a chair watching the news on T.V., his brandy on a small side stool, smoke rose from his cigarette.

"What is it, my dear?" he asked, graciously.

"Dad…" I hesitated, "I really want to go…"

"Go where?" he asked. I wondered if he knew what I meant but was acting oblivious.

"To America," I said. "I already told my teachers that I'm leaving after O-levels."

"Like I said, Ms. Kautsire, finish your A-levels first, then America will come next."

I sulked harder. "But Trevor says I can start college instead of A-levels."

"No. A-levels first. Then we'll talk America," he reached for his brandy.

Tears formed in my eyes. My father sipped his drink.

"You're making me learn things I don't like!" I yelled, "I don't want to be a stupid doctor or a lawyer or whatever!" Tears spilled from my eyes. "I like acting!" I sobbed. "So stop wasting your money!" I sobbed. "And I'm not going back to that school!" I stormed out, slamming the door really hard.

For the whole year, I told people I was going to America. After my O-level exams, of my own free will, I decided to return all my school books to my teachers. It was my way of officiating my goodbyes. In each class, a few others and I, who were leaving Kamuzu Academy, passed around notebooks where our friends wrote goodbye messages. Most of them used my nicknames:

"I will miss you, *Mwanii.*"

"Keep smiling, *Shaguar.*"

"Don't forget me, *Juturna (A.K.A. Audacious One).*"

"Stay fresh, *Ace-Attitude.*"

We also exchanged gifts. Clothes, trinkets, photographs. Anything for memory's sake. It was the end of another school year. Once more, I rode the school bus with my peers, two hours from Kasungu, where our school was located, to Lilongwe airport, where we boarded a plane, forty minutes to Blantyre, where my parents picked me up from Chileka airport. Only this time, they didn't know that I had completely signed off on everything at Kamuzu Academy. I had even given back my uniform. The only thing I took was my green and gold tie, which I stole because we were not allowed to keep them if we were not returning to the school. I had given everything back, never to board school buses and planes with my high school classmates again. Never to return to the Academy. The same Academy I once couldn't wait to get to when I was nine years old and ready to behave like an adult.

*

It took long for Quincy College in Boston to send the paperwork that would allow me to get a student visa from the American embassy. My brothers were our mediators. For months, I watched my father demand answers for why my school I-20 form (a document certifying my eligibility to study in the U.S. as a nonimmigrant student) was taking so long to arrive in Malawi. They always spoke around noon time in Malawi. 6 PM in Boston. One afternoon, when my father had finished his lunch, he sat in the living room. He was wearing a dark gray Pierre Cardin suit, waiting for our houseboy, Dave, to polish his shoes for an afternoon shine. Trevor was on the phone. I was eavesdropping.

"But did you check with Quincy College again?" my father asked Trevor on the phone, frustrated. "It's been months now. We need to get her back to school."

He listened.

"No, not regular mail. It takes too long. Can't they use FedEx or DHL?"

He listened.

"I faxed all the bank letters and affidavit forms they requested. There should be no problem."

He listened.

"Okay. Check with them again and keep me posted. And Trevor...make sure they send those papers!" he demanded.

These were the conversations they had for almost six months. But this only added to the disappointment my father had already felt. Since I had left Kamuzu Academy without his approval, he had been upset with me. He had only found out about my plans to not return when a new school year was about to begin at the Academy. Three months before these conversations with Trevor began, I was watching T.V. in my room, when my father called my name from his bedroom. I jumped from my bed and rushed into the corridor. His bedroom door was open, and I could see him through the corner crack, seated on his favorite chair with his legs crossed at the knees, watching the news. I knocked.

"*Lowa!*" he said.

I walked in and stood by the door.

"How much money do you need for school grocery shopping?" he asked.

I swallowed hard. "I don't need any," I said in a soft low voice, petrified of a conversation I had been dreading.

"What? What do you mean you don't need any?" His face looked puzzled as if I had said something unfathomable.

I looked to the side, avoiding eye contact. "I returned my school books and uniform. I told you I'm not going back."

"I beg your pardon?" He gave me a hard stare. Very little blinking.

"I returned all my stuff. I told the school I'm not going back." My right hand touched the wall.

He readjusted himself on his chair. "And…who told you to do that?" His tone was shifting to furious sarcasm. I was familiar with that voice. "Did I say you could do that?"

No response. I looked toward the T.V. screen, avoiding his confrontational stare.

"Young lady, school is important. Stop messing yourself up!" he shouted. "You will go back to Kamuzu Academy and you will complete your A-levels!"

"But I want to go to America," I whined.

"There will be no America until you finish here!"

"But…"

"I said you are going back!" he shouted, pointing his finger at me.

I ran off to cry in my room.

At first, I sulked for days. Barely spoke to my father. We passed each other in the corridor as if we were strangers. No eye contact. My mother tried to console me whenever she found me sulking in my room. I would lay my head on her lap.

Sometimes, I sobbed as she gently stroked my hair back, trying to get me to understand why my father was being indifferent.

"He's just worried that you're not interested in school anymore," she said.

"*I am*, Ma. I just don't want to go back to K.A. There's nothing there for me. Trevor said I could start college, remember?"

"Yes, but what will you do while we sort out school papers? Those things take time."

"I don't know...but I'm not going back to K.A."

My mother continued to give me reports of my father's concerns. Once, she told me he feared that I would stay an undereducated girl who would end up pregnant and rush into an unwanted marriage. I realized that my choice to leave K.A. had made my father doubt that we shared the same values—to be an educated and independent individual. Looking back, if we had talked about it, if we had really listened to each other, we would have realized we had the same goals in mind. But being young, avoiding him felt like a louder, dramatic way of communicating how unhappy I was about my life in Malawi.

My father had to cave in. Three months had gone by and he couldn't bear to see me doing nothing at home, fearing that my brain would go dull. Correspondence with Trevor about Quincy College went in full swing when one magical day, my father said to Trevor at the end of their phone conversation in the dining room during lunch time: "Trevor, we need to do something about your sister." My mother and I were still having our lunch. We immediately exchanged glances, smiling, but still trying to conceal that we were eavesdropping. My father never said anything to me after that, but I knew hope for an academic future had resurfaced. Soon we started talking again, usually about where he was in the process of my school application. Each time he made progress faxing a document to Quincy College or getting a confirmation from them, he reported it to me. He knew America was all I was living for at that time. Coincidentally, Charles had also suggested I learn how to use the computer, basic Microsoft programs, Word, Excel, PowerPoint. He told us that unlike the Academy, where most of our assignments were hand-written, people used computers to do their school work in America.

"You can't start college in America without knowing how to use a computer. You do everything on a computer here," Charles said.

When I relayed the news to my father, he was ecstatic. His daughter would have a temporary purpose. I would be learning something again while waiting for Quincy College to send all the necessary school documents. This would pacify his concern about my idleness at home. At sixteen, I learned how to use Microsoft computer programs. It was perfect timing. Because the following year, by the time a professor gave me an essay assignment to be done on a Word document, I was more than ready to tackle Microsoft. I would be an international student with one less thing to be culture-shocked about in America.

Kalo

More than thirty male and female gardeners worked for "Lily of the Valley," my mother's flower company. They were my guardians—always making sure I was inside our yard by 5 PM. Like my mother, they also taught me how to cook nsima on firewood and they influenced my taste for delicacies like dried fish, okra, birds, grasshoppers, and *mbewa* (mice). Malawians find roasted mice delicious. Add salt and pepper, and munch on them like beef jerky— definitely an acquired taste. I was very fond of our workers because they told me stories about their lives, the adversities of village life. They were also newscasters for hot, neighborhood gossip: "Kalo, guess who got caught sleeping with another man's wife?" "Kalo, guess who got fired yesterday?" "Kalo, another woman got cursed by a witchdoctor!" "Kalo, guess who the current neighborhood whore is?" Their pronunciation of Carol as "Kalo" communicated their affection and a casual, playfulness that allowed them to butcher the consonants in my name with Malawian phonetics. "Kalo" was comfortable in both sound and sentiment. Young workers, ranging from ages 18 to late-20s, talked about unrequited love or conquests with people they fancied. They shared how their desires to get an education were destroyed by unexpected pregnancies, sickness or no funds. Older workers talked about jobs and marriage problems. Sometimes, I worked with them in my mother's garden, of my own will, because my world grew larger when I heard about their problems. Our lives were so different, but they also gave me hints that there was more to life than the one I was living.

One gardener, a man in his late 40s, worked for us during the day and as an overnight guard somewhere else. We called him Mani. He was tall, slim, dark-skinned and had a muscly body. His eyes were always red, probably from sleep deprivation or the tobacco he smoked. Whenever I asked him why he looked exhausted, he said having no sleep was a sign—a reminder—that he was making money to provide for his family. I couldn't imagine how anybody could carry heavy tools and cut grass with a scythe without sleep. But lack of sleep was *his* normal, he said. Sometimes, I wanted to tell him to go lie down somewhere and that I wouldn't tell anyone he was sleeping. But I also knew I would be letting my mother down because she wasn't paying over thirty workers for someone to sleep on the job. Every time Mani saw me in the yard, he would nod his head and give a tired smile. I would do the same, only my smile was always filled with guilt. I knew there was something I couldn't help him with, something he claimed as his normal sign of virtue in being a man, a husband, and father.

Another middle-aged worker struggled with alcohol addiction. His name was Gomani. He told me humorous stories about spending all his salary at a bar. Sometimes my parents talked about his habit when warning me and my brothers about the dangers of alcohol. Gomani avoided confronting his reckless behavior by complaining about his wife. At times, his speech was so slurred that I couldn't understand his Chichewa. He often reeked of booze. I reckon *his* normal was coming to work drunk.

"She locked me outside again, Kalo! So cruel," then he would mumble. His eyes, bloodshot. Thick white saliva crusted at the sides of his mouth. "Because…do you know what that meant? Hmm?" he sounded like a drunk teacher with a rhetorical question, waiting for an answer from his student, "No sex, Kalo! All night! Imagine!" he would shout while clapping his hands and shaking his head as if he had just experienced a tragic loss. I laughed with him, but I didn't want to imagine anything sexual about him. Instead, I worried for his wife. I wondered what kind of woman would stay with a man who spent his entire salary at a bar. Village women always seemed more confrontational with men. I had seen a few of them yell at their husbands just like black women on American television. Only sometimes their husbands would retaliate and beat them—both indoors and in public. Love is blind in the villages, too, and my mind swarmed with questions when Gomani complained about no sex. Maybe she had nowhere else to go. Maybe she was settling, finding it easier to stay with Gomani than starting over alone. At times, I waited for Gomani to say she had left him for good, but he kept returning with the same story. Each time, blaming his wife for withholding sex. Sometimes he threatened to cheat because of the locked door. But with his constant drunken state, who knew if he had already done it.

Yet, Gomani also had good qualities. He was a reliable worker, thoughtful too. *He* was the man we always found working the hardest in the garden. *He* was the man my parents trusted to make sure I was home before dark. *He* was the man who could work long hours if my mother needed him to. *He* was the man that picked guavas and mangoes from our garden so I didn't have to climb trees. *He* was the man who never whined about his job. *He* was the man who made everyone laugh with stories about his misfortunes, even though his justifications were somewhat skewed. I will never forget the last company New Year's Eve party that my mother threw before I moved to America. Gomani was notorious for passing out from drinking too much. But that night he danced to Malawian music for as long as he could.

"Kalo, come! Let's dance! You will never see dancing like this in America!" he said, swinging his hips, trying to steady himself. "White people don't know how to dance!" he shouted, taking small steps this way and that like someone trying to escape hot coals under their feet. Mphatso and I had made a bet that he wouldn't make it until the new year. But Gomani danced and danced, making everyone laugh with dance moves from Mars. He looked like a baby in diapers, legs stuck to the ground, slightly bent, only able to swing his hips. By 11 PM, Gomani was lying in a corner covered in urine—the result of mixing an African sorghum beer called *Chibuku* with "Malawi Gin" (which Gomani called "aluminum" because he thought the drink was as strong as aluminum used to build planes). That was the first time I ever saw a grown man pee on himself. I couldn't imagine living a life like Gomani's, but the way he shifted between good and bad habits made me realize the complexity in people. Here was a debauched man lying in his own piss, a man who was also good at his job, a man whom unlike Mani spent his entire salary on booze instead of family, a man who would later caution me about prostitution in America.

*

For weeks, I pestered the gardeners about the new life I would live in the United States. A few days before my trip to America, we sat in the garden, in a big circle of about ten people, others were scattered around the same area. Women wore t-shirts with skirts, chitenjes wrapped around their waists, and scarves tied around their heads. Men wore shorts, trousers, or green company overalls, a few of them had unbuttoned shirts and some were shirtless. We were filling black soil in black plastic bags where new plants would grow. It was a hot stuffy day, and I had just eaten nsima, vegetables, and dried fish with them. The gardeners enjoyed eating with me, but they always wondered what kind of girl would want to eat food from the villages rather than what they assumed was always fancy food from the house. Dave knew to inform my parents that I wouldn't join them for lunch. My parents had no problem with this because they liked that I had an open mind about socializing and eating with our workers. I imagine they were relieved that they weren't raising a pompous child.

I made noise in the garden.

"You'll see me on T.V. with James Bond!" I shouted, moving around the circle like a spy, using my finger as a gun to shoot at plants.

"Sure, Kalo!" they laughed. "But we better not find you in blue movies!" someone shouted. Loud cackling laughter followed. I plopped myself on the ground, laughing with everyone. Then, I reassured them that I wouldn't do pornographic movies. There was more laughter, a few women chattered, staring at me with comically doubtful faces. One woman chuckled so loud, we could see the big gap between her teeth, "*Wabodza iwe!*" she said, calling me a liar. We laughed some more. Then topics switched like a fast improv show—an unexpected roast of Kalo took place. They jested about me eating food that wouldn't satisfy my hunger the way nsima did.

"You are going to ask your mother to FedEx nsima and chicken stew every month!" We laughed. One woman stood up because her chitenje was coming undone, "Njala n'chilombo!" she shouted, wiping sweat from her forehead with her chitenje. A famous Malawian metaphor—"Hunger is like an animal." I knew they were joking about FedExing cooked nsima, but I still told them it was impossible to do that. Just in case.

"What about *Kuminula*?" asking if I would start wearing short, tight mini-skirts and if I would show off my long legs without worrying about being mocked by vendors. I said, maybe. Then I explained that, unlike Malawians, Americans were more open to miniskirts.

"Just don't become a prostitute, Kalo!" Gomani shouted, cackling with his head back.

We laughed some more. Some clapped their hands. Others said I would start dating white men and have mixed babies.

"You are going to change the color of the family, Kalo," a woman who looked in her late forties shouted. I don't remember her name, but she was the quietest. She had sun-dried skin and a sad smile, the kind that looks like someone withholding pain. I told them that Whites could be just as good-looking as Blacks, so my family would benefit from Jensen Ackles' gorgeous genes. And, yes, they knew about my crush on Mr. Ackles, too. Our workers also thought of Whites as superior to Blacks. They even referred to anything fancy as *za chizungu,* "things for white people." Their white supremacist logic was similar to my high school friend, Agnes, who once told me that I wouldn't be cast in movies in America because I was not white—symptoms of how deeply rooted distorted western ideas lurked in some people. I never tried to school our gardeners on race. Back then, I didn't think they cared. They seemed set in the lives they were living, in their beliefs—even if it meant accepting inferiority in society. And I admit that at that time, I didn't have enough knowledge about race. I didn't know the proper language or ways to address it. Our gardeners were humble and their stories showed me how much bigger the world was. They showed me how having very little in their lives made them appreciate things more. I wanted to have a heart that appreciates, too, and I wondered if I would find other people like them in America. In all our jesting, I knew they understood that I would adopt a new identity, that I would become someone different from the "Kalo" they knew.

Ms. Kautsire

A wooden half-naked male hunter holding a spear and a
shield—bulging eyeballs, a big nose with a dark brown
mole the size of a marble, his nostrils flaring open, as if fire
could blaze out of them at any moment, mouth agape with
big chiseled teeth—this would be the last I would see of the
Ngoni tribe sculpture that stood in our living room. He
looked vicious, judgmental of anyone who passed through
the living room. I was greeted by his stare each day.
Sometimes I averted my eyes as I scurried past, fearing it
might come to life and confront me. I often imagined it
reprimanding me with its glare. Whether I had been
mischievous or not, it would disapprove of my behavior,
how I carried myself, banging its spear against the
shield, "This is not the proper behavior of a Malawian girl,"
it would say in our Chichewa language. I envisioned it as a
chief, summoning tribal spirits to roam around our living
room in the middle of the night—performing peculiar
rituals, witchcraft. Why? I don't know. But my mind veered
there. Because Malawi had traditions I did not fully
understand. I always wondered why anyone would want
frightening art in their house? But these questions
wouldn't matter anymore. I was seventeen years old and

about to move to America. Surely Boston houses would not have any half-naked judgmental sculptures adorning their living rooms.

*

I had been the subject of a family meeting on the night before I departed for Boston. Our custom was to gather together in the living room to discuss trips made outside of Malawi. My father said my grandmother introduced this tradition whenever he traveled away. Even when he was married to my mother and was no longer under my grandmother's roof, he was always summoned for a talking-to like a child. My stubborn grandmother needed to drill my father with discipline before departure. This send-off would remind him of the values and responsibilities my grandmother had taught him. When my older brothers left for Boston years before me, they also had family meetings. I don't remember what was talked about when Trevor had his because I was too young. And I missed Charles's meeting because I was in boarding school at Kamuzu Academy. On the night of February 3rd, 2004, my father decided to hold my meeting after dinner in our living room. The wooden sculpture of a half-naked Ngoni hunter with a spear and shield would be present too.

I sat on our brown tweed couch, waiting for my parents to join me, looking around the living room as though everything in our house was unfamiliar—the big chandelier hanging at the center of the room, the rectangular glass tables below it, my mother's driftwood flower arrangements, how my brothers and I looked so young in framed photographs. Then, my mind flashed to Boston. I imagined what my brothers' apartment would look like. It would soon be my new home. Quite frankly, my mind could only land on what I had seen on Will Smith's T.V. show, *Fresh Prince of Bel-Air*: a living room with an open concept that led to the kitchen at one end and the front door at the other. Of course, there would be no British butler to announce when we had guests as they did for the Fresh Prince. That would actually be more like my present house in Malawi because we did have our cook, Dave, who would kneel in the kitchen or living room to announce each guest we received.

When my parents joined me in the living room, we sat on separate sofas so we could face each other. My father had his Premier Brandy on one of the glass tables, his usual night cap before bed. My mother sat on a sofa next to him, already in her nightgown and head-wrap, her arms folded around her body, waiting for her turn to speak. My father began.

"Carol, *Mwakula!* You are a big girl now. *Ife,* we've done our part and now you have to be responsible for yourself."

My palms grew sweaty, my body fluctuated between excitement and nervousness.

"Like your brothers, you begged and begged and begged to go to America for your studies," he smiled, looking at me.

I smiled too, thinking of the relentlessness it took to beg a father who had other plans for my education. The way he persuaded me to be a doctor or a lawyer when I wanted to become an actress. The way he pressured me to do my A-levels at Kamuzu Academy when I wanted to begin college after O-levels. I broke eye contact and looked at the hardwood floor instead.

"You have convinced me, Ms. Kautsire." He spoke with so many pauses you would think he was William Shatner's brother. But I suspected that it was hard for my father to let go of his only daughter. "Go and get the college education you want." He paused. "*Ine*, all I ask from you is hard work." Pause. "Do not waste my money doing bugger-all." Pause. "America is a world that belongs to other people." Pause. "Behave yourself." Pause. "And as I always say, when in Rome, do as the Romans do." Maybe he was searching for the right words to say to me, maybe he was choking up with emotions.

My father said he was proud that I was the kind of girl who wanted to pursue college. To him, my interest in education meant there was still a chance that I was going to be a doctor or a lawyer. And I sat, listening to him imagine me as an intelligent, successful, and independent woman. Everything he wanted me to be. I observed my mother. There was sadness on her face. At times, her eyes were fixed on the hardwood floor too. She looked distant as if she was imagining me already in America. Or maybe she was thinking about my absence in the house. I spent most of my teen years in boarding school, so leaving my parents was not a new or frightening thing for me. Yet unlike leaving for high school in Kasungu, moving to America would be different because I wouldn't be able to return for a vacation after every three months. We hadn't even discussed when I would return for a visit. For weeks before the family meeting, I found myself looking at my mother's face and feeling the emptiness build in my heart. I felt sorry for us. Since age nine, boarding school had separated us. The two-to-three week holidays were all we had to keep our mother-daughter bond alive. And now, at age seventeen, I was leaving her again, and this time—for years. I felt as if life had robbed me of time to connect with my mother, as if we only knew each other in passing, between school and holidays. I grew desperate for ways to muffle the loud thoughts of distress about leaving the most important woman in my life. When her time came to speak, she only said a few words.

"You've heard what your father has said… and I hope you realize how important it is. *Ife*, we are very proud of you, Carol, and we wish you well."

Tears welled up. My palms were clammy and I opened my eyes as wide as possible and blinked hard—a method I often used to push back tears.

My father continued. "We have talked about all your immigration documents. We have gone through each of them one by one. Keep them safe." Pause. "And Ms. Kautsire…" He looked directly at me, smiling, his fingers intertwined, eyes red. I could swear if he blinked, tears would roll.

"Make sure you follow the signs at the airports. Do not get lost."

Going to America

My eyelids gently opened, letting in the morning sun. It was February 4th, 2004, the day I would leave Malawi. I stared at my bedroom ceiling and a big smile followed my realization that the agony of waiting for time to bring me closer to America had finally come to an end. I flung my pink blanket as far from my body as possible and ran into the corridors like a child eager to catch Santa sneaking in presents. I wondered if my mother and father were awake and just as excited for me as I was. I ran down the corridor, passing the half-naked Ngoni sculpture, flinging the kitchen door open with a massive grin. There was no one in the kitchen. I was only greeted by the humming sound of the fridge. A flask of coffee was set at the side of the stove and some mugs had been placed on a tray, so this told me that someone had been there. Someone somewhere was awake and I needed their acknowledgment to celebrate my life-changing day. I rushed back to the bedrooms, quickly glancing at the clock in the corridor. The hand of the clock pointed at the hour of six and I knew my mother would be up. My parents were both early birds, and almost every day my father attended six o'clock mass at church. I knocked eagerly on their bedroom door.

"*Lowa!* The door is unlocked!" my mother shouted.

I opened the door and ran towards her dresser where she powdered her face with her favorite Mac makeup. I gave her a hug. For a few seconds, we exchanged glances without words. I let my beaming grin speak for itself. The smile asked an unspoken question of my mother: *Are you as excited as I am?* And her reciprocal smile was her warm response to my curiosity.

"The wait is finally over! *Ndiye kusangalalatu,*" she said. Her face was glowing. She seemed proud, very happy that her daughter's dream to go to America to become an actress was finally coming true. I would become the consolation for the chance she lost to study acting. My grin grew wider. I held her tightly, lingering in our embrace.

"So you are going to be a film actress?" she asked with a warm giggle, "You have no fear?"

I shook my head, still holding her. "No, Ma. You know how crazy I am. I'm not scared."

We both laughed.

She asked if everything was packed and if I had had breakfast. I told her I was too excited to eat. I was just as eager to get to America as I was when my parents first drove me to Kamuzu Academy. Only I doubted that I could travel all the way to Boston without eating. She asked if I was excited to see Disney World, a place she had often spoke about after her trips to America. I said yes, but that I didn't know when I would begin traveling from state to state. We laughed about childish fantasies of Mickey Mouse and Cinderella waiting to sing for me when I arrived at the airport—how I would bump into famous musicians and movie stars. Maybe Beyoncé or Will Smith would invite me over for dinner one day. We joked around a lot that morning, but every time we caught each other's stare, there was something about the way we shook our heads, the way my mother looked down at whatever makeup tool or product she was holding in her hands. I knew what it was because I felt it, too. We had been in this situation before but, this time, Lieutenant Mother wouldn't fire questions about what kind of girl I was for being excited to leave home. This time, she seemed more accepting of my new reality. This time, we glanced at each other with a mutual struggle—the struggle to appear strong because of my new journey to America, when deep down, our worlds were collapsing because of our separation.

*

I dragged my packed suitcases from my bedroom, past the corner of the living room with the wooden half-naked Ngoni sculpture, past the television in the living room, past the white fridge. I stopped in the kitchen to look at the brown spice cabinets, next to them was the war zone I once hated—the stove. *No more blisters.* I smirked at the stove as if it knew my thoughts. I dragged both my large suitcase and a small carry-on out of the kitchen door. Dave asked if he could help me with anything, but I was too excited to stop for anyone's assistance. I did all the packing and carrying myself. The more I moved things alone, the more I was taking it all in. Help from someone else would have felt like minimizing the significance of my move to America.

"I'll carry it myself," I chortled while charging past Dave, struggling to stabilize my tiny body, extending each arm behind me as straight as possible so that I could lead each suitcase in the right direction. When I reached my father's Peugeot 605, I lifted the larger suitcase handle to my chin, inching each footstep near the car trunk so that I could place it in carefully. Someone stronger than normally loaded anything heavy in the car, but on this occasion, I chose to do it alone. A few gardeners who were weeding the lawn near the gate looked at me as though I were insane. Some of them waved, others raised their trowels high, smiling at me from ear to ear. I waved back, both hands in the air. No more Kalo to cook nsima with.

*

At the backseat of my father's Peugeot, I rolled down the window as the car pulled out of our gate. My father was driving. He put on some classical music, and my mother sat quietly in the passenger seat. I wanted to inhale the air in the streets of Sunny Side one more time, a part of me wishing my body could store Malawian atmosphere to carry with me to America, a memory of where I am from. Yet, another part of me was eager to detach from Malawi because this chapter of my life was not destined for its grounds. At the back of my mind, I knew that moving to America meant becoming someone else, and I was curious to find out. I stuck my arm outside the window to feel the cool breeze brushing against my skin, sliding through the spaces between my fingers. I reached for everything I saw. Big brick houses. Muddied white servants' quarters. Grass lawns, some with a few brown patches. Tall brick fences. Straw fences, some falling off, exposing big yards. Tar-marked roads. Dirt roads with protruding rocks that often shook our cars vigorously. Memories of days when I ran barefoot to and from friends' houses flashed in my head. I thought of the games we played—*rounder's*, fly-ball, *bhula*, hide and seek, army games. The kicks and punches I endured in fighting contests, the dangerous bike challenges that left me bleeding for acceptance. Those days would be left behind. Simon's "big female boy" was moving out of town, and the giant scar on my right shoulder was coming with me. In America, maybe it could even pass for a tattoo.

As my father turned the corner of Smythe road, where my Aunt Rose lived, I remembered the day my mother and I saw a thief hiding in the leaves as we drove past it one night. When my mother took the same turn, the car headlights lit up the corner, and a layer of leaves suddenly lifted up. A face peered through, then the pile of leaves swiftly fell back down. We both shrieked. My heart raced, fearing we were about to get ambushed.

"Eh-eh! Did I just see a person lying there?" my mother asked. Then her mouth stayed agape with fright.

"Yes, someone is hiding there," I whispered, holding on to the dashboard. I looked around to see if a team of men would appear to surround our car.

"Waiting to rob someone, I bet!" my mother chuckled.

"Ma, just drive fast, please." Unlike my mother who was quick to calm herself, I was still struck with fear. My imagination was already unleashing images of shadows with machetes. Nightmares manifested quickly for me—the effects of a six-year-old's trauma from a house robbery. Since my Aunt Rose lived next to Smythe road, she often told my mother and me about people getting robbed if it started to get dark outside. She and her family heard people screaming for help. Other neighbors said if they had a guard, they would try to intervene, but if there was none, they would fear getting harmed too. There was no choice but to listen to or block out cries for help. *I hope America is safer,* I thought, as our car moved further away from the frightful corner on Smythe Road. The only fear that lingered was for my family and friends.

*

We drove past a series of apartment complexes where one of my first crushes lived. I only saw the entrance, a huge green gate with wheels, adjacent to the tall grass in the sides of the roads that led to it. I kissed a boy there. We did a lot of it actually. His name was Maziko. I pictured it again. I was wearing black jeans with a green shirt, my hair was tied in a bun but it was messy and my baby hairs were sticking out. He wore baggy jean shorts, an oversized t-shirt and he had cornrows that completed his resemblance to the rapper, Lil Bow Wow. That was also the nickname I gave him whenever I spoke about him with my friends. I remembered the confidence in his smile, and how he slowly moved his face closer to mine for a deep kiss. He was gentle with his tongue but knew when to be rough. I enjoyed kissing Maziko. Sometimes, he left me speechless— Caroline undone. And my kissing technique got better and better. I couldn't wait to kiss an American boy. Maybe I still

209

had time to hook up with Jensen Ackles. I smiled again as the car drove past the green gate next to the tall grass.

Saying goodbye to Blantyre City was a sharp awakening. Since it was morning, the streets were not crowded with people yet. The town already felt strangely unfamiliar as I took mental pictures of everything I wanted to remember, memories of what the town represented. A shop called "People's Trading Center" (P.T.C.) which was a popular hangout spot for most teenagers. A white brick building complemented with blue and red lines and "P.T.C." logos. Since the age of thirteen, this was where my friends and I bought cookies, crisps, and candy; alcohol, too. We had no concern for things like a legal drinking age. In Malawi, if you could afford it, you could buy it. P.T.C. was also where we were likely to bump into boys we had crushes on. When we told our parents we were "going into town," we meant more than going to buy a few things. We were going fishing for boys we liked. Coincidentally, my father met and pursued my mother when she was working at P.T.C. I wondered if America had shops that were popular courting zones. Next, we drove past "National Bank of Malawi," where I often insisted on accompanying my mother and father for one reason—a stop at the bank meant I could ask them for money. The chances of refusal were low. There would be no more of this, no free money, and no easy access to parental ATMs in America. Then there was "Bata," where I bought most of my black school shoes and white running sneakers for primary school. The countless times I made my father return shoes I didn't like, threatening that I wouldn't go to school if I wasn't wearing black shoes with laces, instead of black Mary Janes. These landmarks carried my youth, and driving past them made me realize the kind of freedom and privileges I took for granted, things that only became clear because I was leaving Malawi. Everything was going to be different in America, and by the time we drove past a town called Chirimba, I saw something else I was leaving behind. Something that conjured guilt.

Deterioration. It was all over the houses in the streets of Chirimba. Of course there were a few big brick houses with beautiful yards, but they were among mud houses and poorly designed buildings. Many of the houses were built so close to each other with barely any space between them. In the morning, the streets were quiet. Stray dogs roamed around and a few kids in tattered clothes wandered the streets near the marketplaces, which were also right next to people's homes. The space had no plot design or organization to help make sense of which space belonged to whom. Sometimes, parts of buildings looked displaced, the roofs of small shops either had old metal plates falling off or thick plastics pressed down by giant rocks (probably to stop their plastic roofs from blowing away). Street vendors sold food and clothes along the same streets. Everything looked cluttered. The sight began to upset me. I stopped looking outside the window. My thoughts fled from the poverty in front of me to America. *Will I find places like this in America?* I knew about the ghetto that rappers sang about, scenes from movies, but I couldn't imagine how real it was. After all, Hollywood was known to exaggerate things. I couldn't even imagine a vendor chasing a car to ask the driver for money in America. *Forget about poverty. You're going to a first world country now.* But, I couldn't shake off the feeling. I felt guilty for the privilege to go to America when people in my country were suffering. I felt as if I was getting away with something, an opportunity that was not fair to others, a situation I could not fix, but feel concern for. Maybe what bothered me was why thieves broke into our house when I was six.

"Almost there, Ms. Kautsire!" my father announced, looking at me through the rear view mirror.

I smiled.

The car moved fast. I tried to leave worry behind.

*

Several long lines were formed from the entrance of the airport building to individual checkout desks. I placed my suitcase on the table for scanning and security check. My mother and I watched the contents of my bag on a screen that was being inspected. Mostly clothes, a few books, and school documents. I had used a chocolate brown chitenje to cover the contents of my suitcase so they wouldn't move around a lot. It was the only chitenje I liked. It had no intricate patterns, it was less colorful and the fabric was soft. Taking it with me made my mother happy. I would have a piece of Malawi with me. When I walked through the metal detector, my heart skipped a beat as if I had stolen something, but it was just my nerves—an inherent free-floating paranoia that built up when an authority figure wanted to search for anything illegal.

The room was humming with sounds, talking people, beeping machines, airport clerks stamping documents. My father joined me and my mother on the line. Most travelers were older men and women. Some women wore traditional African attires. They stood comfortably in layers of colorful fabric, their head-wraps tied in creative shapes I could not understand. I didn't know what they were expressing with the twisting, folding and knotting of their fabric. Everyone else wore regular clothes. I wondered if any of them were going to America too. No one looked my age. I had questions about what kind of parents would let their seventeen-year-old child travel to a distant land—alone? Were they wondering if they were insane, too? Since there was no one my age, I searched for kind faces instead. Maybe I could make friends. I could strike a conversation with someone and make my trip more exciting and less lonely. But I had doubts about applying my social skills in other countries. I knew how to talk to people in Malawi, but I had never been to other countries other than South Africa. A weekend with people from Johannesburg was not enough to understand what works or not when interacting with strangers. Maybe I was better off keeping to myself.

My mother stared at my face as I panned the room. She looked serene, but her eyes moved as if she was reading me like a book. You would think she was looking at a stranger. I didn't know what to make of it because my mother was good at looking relaxed even at a time of crisis. Here was a mother who was possibly panicking about my trip, falling into depression that her last born child was leaving her. Her future—another empty childless house. My father seemed calm, but his smoking gave away his anxiety—the way he inhaled smoke more deeply than other times he had smoked. He fidgeted a lot too, constantly tugging at the waist of his trousers, readjusting, pulling them up when they weren't even falling down. I also suspected he expressed his emotions through his strict cautions—half-serious remarks about traveling with drugs, and luggage anxieties: "Ms. Kautsire, I hope you didn't take any maize flour because security might think it's cocaine;" "Ms. Kautsire, don't take too many things, your luggage will be overweight. Buy new things in America;" "Ms. Kautsire, carry a piece of paper with the Boston address. Americans might think you are homeless. Show them you know where you are going." My mother and I always laughed, dismissing him as a nervous Nellie. These were moments when the tiny snake-survivor with guts disappeared and a man filled with fear emerged. Maybe these were the same things my bad-ass grandmother warned him about. But I couldn't imagine her as an anxious woman. If anything, my grandmother would be the only black woman standing in a corner, puffing her cigarette with pride, sending me off to America in the same way she welcomed me into the world the day I was born—with smoke. Yet where documents were required, I appreciated my father's endless inquiries about having the right papers and packing lightly. Because that day, my luggage was not overweight, I knew where I was going and the airport clerks saw nothing suspicious about me. I had four printed electronic tickets. One: Blantyre to Johannesburg, Two: Johannesburg to Nairobi. Three: Nairobi to Amsterdam. Four: Amsterdam to Boston. A trip that would take a day and a half.

*

I had told myself I wouldn't cry at the airport. The excitement would put out the homesickness that threatened to consume me. It was time to enter the travelers lounge. My parents and I stood at the door—the cusp that would separate us for two years, maybe more. I hugged my father.

"Ah, Ms. Kautsire. Safe journey. Good luck," he said. His usual semi-formal words during vulnerable moments. No tears.

My mother was not a crier either, so I didn't expect it. I hugged her. First, a tight squeeze. Then, we stood in silence, still hugging. I didn't want to let go. And my mother wasn't letting go either. My heart was sinking. My mind was screaming: *I'm sorry, Mom. I'm so sorry that I'm leaving again.* Then, she whispered many things in my ear, "God bless you," "I will miss you," "Be a good girl," "I love you very much." Her voice was soft, slightly raspy.

"I'll miss you too, Ma," I said, a lump of pain building in my throat. I opened my eyes as wide as possible, fluttering my blinks to push back tears. We let each other go.

*

Time sped up. In the passenger's lounge, I took deep breaths to ground myself. Loneliness set in. Now on my own, the thought of the distance to America triggered a fright that made it seem like I could not function at airports. My legs stiffened, my arms were shaky and wobbly as if I was slowly getting paralyzed. More deep breaths. I identified my luggage outside the lounge, showed my ticket to a flight attendant who then tore part of it and gave me the section I needed to identify my seat. I walked towards the plane. There was a balcony where people could watch passengers board the plane. My parents were on the left end, waving. They had already spotted me. At the sight of them, a sudden wave of emotion filled every fiber of my being. I felt like I was going to collapse. Tears began to flow. All my efforts to push back tears rendered useless. These were tears without warning—a spontaneous overflow of emotions I had tried to subdue for weeks. I wiped them off. But more came down. Another flight attendant welcomed me on board with an enthusiastic smile. I grinned trying to hide any signs of crying. She pointed me towards my seat and I sauntered my way through the aisle, constantly tugging at my suitcase. *You are okay, Carol, you are okay. This is the life you wanted.* I had to keep telling myself. I placed my suitcase in the luggage compartment above my seat. I sat down and buckled up. The seat felt unusual. My body, out of place. This was not home, and I was on my way to a place very unfamiliar.

I was now hyperventilating. My parents were nowhere in sight. All I could see outside my window was dry grass and a runway. My heart was shattering as tears poured. I saw flashes of my mother's sad yet strong face, looking at the plane she was trusting to carry her daughter safely from one destination to the next. My father's serious expression, concealed concern, looking attentively at the plane that would sweep me away to a land where he could not teach, caution or scold me. No more father-daughter car rides. My childhood faded each second I drew closer to departure. Voices echoed in my head.

Mom: "A film actress? You have no fear?"

Dad: "Do not get lost."

Agnes: America is for white people. You're black!"

Gomani: "Just don't become a prostitute, Kalo!"

Mom: "Be a good girl."

Dad: "Ms. Kautsire…show them you know where you're going."

Then, the sound of a beep. The captain announced flight details, hopeful of a smooth journey because the weather was clear. Flight attendants did their signal routine of Do's and Don'ts, pointing at emergency exits.

"Please fasten your seatbelts, and we'll prepare for takeoff," the captain concluded.

I held onto the handles of my seat, eyes shut, then I went to my happy place—envisioning America—tall buildings with lights, shiny cars, and glamorous outfits. My mediocre childish fantasy of Mickey Mouse and Cinderella waiting to welcome me with a song at Boston's Logan Airport. An ensemble from the Lion King hailing me like an African Disney Princess. Now *that* made me chuckle. The plane began to move. My heart raced. I gathered the courage to watch our swift swoop across the airport. Then lift off. I saw the tiny verandah where my parents waved until we were so far from the ground of Malawi that they became too small to see. It was time to leave everything behind. I let go of my seat. Leaned my head back. Deep breath. I was flying. Growing up. On my way to find out the kind of girl I would become.